"Elaura Niles reports from the trenches about getting published and getting produced with realism and humor. If you seek success as a writer, save yourself some time, trouble (and maybe a few bucks) by buying *Some Writers Deserve to Starve*."

> —Donald Maass, noted agent and author of *Writing the Breakout Novel*

"Savvy, smart, and practical describe Elaura Niles' advice to book and screenwriters all. Readers of *Some Writers Deserve to Starve* will at last have the insider marketing panache omitted in every other book on the market."

> —Elizabeth Lyon, freelance editor and author of best-selling books on writing

"Writers are literally thrown into the lion's den of the publishing world with no defense. Niles has created a book that not only helps writers break into the publishing world, she makes sure they know what to do and how to behave once they get there."

> —Julie Fast, best-selling author of *Loving Someone With Bipolar Disorder: Understanding and Helping Your Partner*

"In *Some Writers Deserve to Starve*, Elaura Niles provides yet-to-be-published writers with a realistic resource that takes the guess-work out of learning the publishing ropes. Where was she at the beginning of my writing career?!"

—Jennie Shortridge, author of *Riding With the Queen*

"Writers need all the help they can get. Once they write their book the hard work really begins. How do they get their book in print? How do they deal with rejection? What do they do when they are published? Elaura Niles' book is a must-read for all writers who are just starting out and need a road map to learn the terrain. It's also for those who have been there, done that, and need a reminder that an author has no better friend than themselves."

—Richard Vetere, author of *The Third Miracle* and co-author of the screenplay adaptation that was made into a movie produced by Francis Ford Coppola

"I've taught thousands of writers over the years and they all ask the difficult questions that Elaura Niles answers in *Some Writers Deserve to Starve*. Her insights crack the code for wanna-be writers, offering solid information about the publishing business and oh-so-practical protocol for breaking in. It dispels every myth ever heard about this sometimes heartbreaking business and is sensible, sassy, and fun."

—Jessica Morrell, author of *Writing Out the Storm*

SOME WRITERS
DESERVE
TO STARVE

SOME WRITERS
DESERVE
TO STARVE

31 BRUTAL TRUTHS ABOUT THE PUBLISHING INDUSTRY

WRITER'S DIGEST BOOKS
Cincinnati, Ohio
www.writersdigest.com

BY ELAURA NILES

Some Writers Deserve to Starve. Copyright © 2005 by Elaura Niles.
Manufactured in Canada. All rights reserved. No other part of this book may
be reproduced in any form or by any electronic or mechanical means including information storage and retrieval systems without permission in writing
from the publisher, except by a reviewer, who may quote brief passages in a
review. Published by Writer's Digest Books, an imprint of F+W Publications,
Inc., 4700 East Galbraith Road, Cincinnati, Ohio 45236. (800) 289-0963.
First edition.

Visit our Web site at www.writersdigest.com for information on more
resources for writers. To receive a free weekly e-mail newsletter delivering tips
and updates about writing and about Writer's Digest products, register directly at our Web site at http://newsletters.fwpublications.com.

09 08 07 06 05   5 4 3 2 1

Library of Congress Cataloging-in-Publication Data

Niles, Elaura, 1967-
  Some writers deserve to starve : 31 brutal truths about the publishing
industry / by Elaura Niles.
     p. cm.
  Includes index.
  ISBN 1-58297-354-7 (pbk. : alk. paper)
  1. Authorship--Marketing--Handbooks, manuals, etc. 2. Authors and pub-
lishers--Handbooks, manuals, etc. I. Title.
  PN161.N55 2005
  070.5'2--dc22

                                                    2004022917

Edited by: Jane Friedman, Amy Schell
Designed by: Lisa Buchanan-Kuhn
Page layout by: Grace Ring
Production coordinated by: Robin Richie

ve a great manu-
cript, and instead
leaving the event
spired, you wind
feeling intimi-
ted by the seem-
gly insurmount-
le wall of people
ho are already in
e game? It doesn't
em fair. It's not.

DEDICATION

I would like to dedicate this book to all
who have found, and those who will
find, the courage to take the next step.

feel lik
you ar
the ou
lookin
at you
succes
publis
friend
acquai
tances
Have y
ever at
ed a w
ing co
ence, b
signin
literar
gather
knowi

ABOUT THE AUTHOR

Elaura Niles is a former writing conference coordinator who has a big, fat Rolodex. Her years of nonprofit service inspired her to pen an advice book
for writers with her own publishing adventures
(and misadventures) slipped into the pages, too.
Driven by a love of good writing, and socializing,
she continues to be involved with writing communities in the United States and Canada. Visit her
Web site at www.elauraniles.com.

spired, you wind
feeling intimi-
ted by the seem-
gly insurmount-

feel like you are on the outside looking in at your s
cessful, published friends and acquaintances? Have
ever attended a writing conference, book signing or
erary gathering knowing that you have a great ma

TABLE OF CONTENTS

their time on newcomers. And if you do show promise, established authors don't want younger or more
talented scribes vying for jobs and contacts on their

ow this feel-
All too well.
once one of
ose writing
erence writ-
. You know
type. Heart
unding and
manuscript
tched to my
t, I lined up
ring-squad-
yle with two
dozen other
opefuls and
aited for my
minute con-
with a pub-
ning profes-
al. I longed
hear those
agic words,
end the first
ty pages." It
a validation
self-worth.
ward for the
g hours I'd

INTRODUCTION

"WE CANNOT ENTER INTO ALLIANCES UNTIL WE ARE ACQUAINTED WITH THE DESIGNS OF OUR NEIGHBORS."

~Sun-Tzu, *The Art of War*, 500 B.C.

Do you ever feel like you are on the outside looking in at your successful, published friends and acquaintances? Have you ever attended a writing conference, book signing, or literary gathering knowing that you have a great manuscript, and instead of leaving the event inspired, you wind up feeling intimidated by the seemingly insurmountable wall of people who are already in the game? It doesn't seem fair. It's not.

The publishing world is tough to crack. When you are in the early stages of getting people to notice your talent, earning a living through your creative endeavors is like trying to climb Mount Everest with a roll of tooth floss and thumb tacks for spikes. There is no room for amateurs or the ill-equipped. Those already mining wages from this extremely competitive industry don't want to waste their time on newbies. And if you do show promise, established authors don't want younger or more talented scribes vying for jobs and contacts on their turf. The door remains closed to you.

The process of finding someone, other than your mother, who will champion your book takes on the surreal feeling of a high school cafeteria. The popular kids hang out on one side of the room and the dweebs, the nerds, the geeks, the writers … you … cower on the other.

I know this feeling. All too well. I was once one of those writing conference writers. You know the type. Heart pounding and manuscript clutched to my chest, I lined up firing-squad-style with two dozen other hopefuls and waited for my ten-minute consult with a publishing professional. I longed to hear those magic words, "Send the first fifty pages." It was a validation of my self-worth. A reward for the long hours I'd logged on the chair, facing my monitor, pecking away at the keys. More than anything else in the world, I was determined to see my name in print on the cover of a book. I was going to be a world-renowned author. My *New York Times* best-seller was just an agent away. Surely somebody would recognize my talent, spelling errors and all.

This was quite the little fantasy I had playing between my ears. I did get published … eventually. But getting from dreamland to reality, and actually seeing my name in print, was an adventure in discovering the customs of a foreign land (publishing).

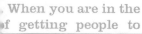
When you are in the f getting people to creative endeavors is climb Everest with a

I learned to keep my networking radar on at all times (you never know who you will meet) and, most of all, face the fact that the mountain I was trying to climb was nothing more than a business (that's right, dollars and cents, profit or loss) to the people who are in the position to promote.

Through my experiences, including a stint as a writing conference coordinator, I met thousands of writers just like me, all longing for their break. And I also found out that there are a series of core truths—truths that writers must learn, accept, and overcome if they hope to make it in publishing. In fact, these truths apply everywhere and to everyone because the industry is a lot like the old high school cafeteria. Especially to you new kids.

Unfortunately, many writers who strive to make an impression on agents and editors aren't aware of the social hierarchies and cutthroat practices that have existed for decades. They are oblivious to the telltale signs that mark them as wanna-bes. Hence, the following truths. I can't guarantee that insider know-how will better your odds, but without it … well, let's just say that you may want to look for an easier occupation like nuclear astrophysics or Olympic water polo.

Remember, this isn't a book on how to write, why to write, or what to write (there are already thousands of those online, in stores, and stacked up on your bookshelves). This is the book that will teach you how to gain acceptance as a professional writer.

their time on newcomers. And if you do show promise, established authors don't want younger or more
talented scribes vying for jobs and contacts on their

ow this feel-
All too well.
once one of
ose writing
rence writ-
. You know
type. Heart
unding and
manuscript
tched to my
t, I lined up
ring-squad-
le with two
dozen other
opefuls and
ited for my
minute con-
with a pub-
ing profes-
al. I longed
hear those
agic words,
nd the first
y pages." It
a validation
self-worth.
vard for the
g hours I'd

SOME STARVING ARTISTS
DESERVE TO STARVE

A novel, a memoir, a short story—whatever you've written—is a magnificent achievement, but, in the beginning, finding a professional who will read your work may seem like a battle. Good. It is a battle. And it all starts with the type of firepower you're packing. As a writer, your No. 1 job is to have the most dynamic book, article, poetry collection, whatever, out there. A professional masterpiece is essential, and anything less than that should not be sent into the fray.

A bit drastic? You bet. I'm a veteran now, but I too was once a novice …

A few years ago, my local library announced a series of evening forums. I was writing my first novel and immediately perked to a session headed by Carolyn Swayze, a literary agent who represents

> "I'm all in favor of keeping dangerous weapons out of the hands of fools. Let's start with typewriters."
> ~Frank Lloyd Wright

William Kinsella (*Shoeless Joe,* which became the classic *Field of Dreams*) and other famous writers. My heart soared. In my humblest opinion, my manuscript was simply magnificent. If I could just find a way to talk to Ms. Swayze privately, tell her my story, I was positive she would want to see the book. I was so convinced of this that I brought all 487 single-spaced, red-inked, coffee-stained pages along with me. There might have been a few misspelled words, run-on sentences, and maybe twenty or thirty thousand extra adverbs, but who needed accuracy when the work was clearly my magnum opus? Surely she would see my Zen brilliance through my occasional spelling errors.

The big night arrived. I secured a front-row seat and was promptly confronted by the motormouthed woman next to me. She was a self-professed "starving artist" with sparkling writing credentials (far more than I had), big dreams (bigger dreams than mine), and a PLAN (I hadn't planned anything beyond being "discovered" by Carolyn that evening). She also had a problem. Fifty thousand of them to be precise. Every one of them owed to a credit card company.

She shared her strategy with me: Cash in on one of those cheesy romance novels. After all, they paid at least $50,000—even for a first book. After paying off her creditors, she would then have enough money left over for a tropical vacation. It would be there on a sandy beach, with the waves crashing in the back-

When you are in the f getting people to

reative endeavors is limb Everest with a

ground, that she would begin her life's work, seize upon her true artistic self and craft deep, meaningful literary prose that would leave the world speechless.

And then Carolyn took her place at the front of the room. Over the next two hours, and to the detriment of motormouth's— and my own—fantasies, Carolyn squelched our misguided notions. She hammered on about how to break into the publishing industry. Who, how, when. Every five minutes she would launch into another "crackpot writer" story. Things NOT to do. Each time I heard the phrase "crackpot writer," my dream had another hole punched in it. Just because I was writing a novel, did that automatically qualify me as one of them, a "crackpot writer"?

Carolyn was very clear that she wasn't going to embrace spelling-challenged manuscripts or notions of big advances for unpublished writers of bodice rippers. That night, in the library's basement lecture hall, I lost my writing virginity and realized I was a "crackpot writer." So was the lady next to me.

THE REALITY
TEST

True or False?

(T) (F) All writers make tons of money.

(T) (F) All writers become respected.

(T) (F) All writers have lovely homes, beautiful
spouses, servants, and they throw Algonquin
Round Table-esque cocktail parties where the
literati bandy about bons mots.

(T) (F) Writing is easy.

(T) (F) Professionalism, content, talent, craft, and
spelling are things a good editor can fix.

**If you answered "true" to any of the above,
go immediately to your nearest community
college and enroll in a program that has a
proven vocation.**

world is toug
to crack. Whe
you are in th
early stages
getting peopl
to notice you
talent, earnir
a living
through you
creative
endeavors is
like trying to
climb Everes
with a roll of
tooth floss an
thumb tacks
for spikes.
There is no
room for ama
teurs or the i
equipped.
Those alread
mining wage
from this
extremely co
petitive indus
try don't war
to waste thei
time on new-
comers. And
you do show
promise, esta
lished autho
don't want
younger or
more talente
scribes vying

PUTTING WORDS ON A PAGE DOES NOT
OBLIGATE ANYONE TO READ THEM

Unfortunately, this day and age has produced a sense of entitlement among creative types, including writers. To live in a first-world country is to be born with the inalienable right to reap huge rewards for a minimal amount of effort. As we become adults, many of us get sucked into those you-can-do-it cheerleading infomercials and then, somewhere along the way, decide that just because we've found the courage to show up at the page and jot down a few words, we will be published.

It takes more than that. It takes dedication, commitment to craft, and in some rash cases, tens of thousands of dollars of credit card debt. Is that enough? I wish.

The old adage says that if you stay in the game long enough, the number of rivals will thin and you

"Thank you for sending me a copy of your book—I'll waste no time reading it."
~Moses Hadas

will eventually be victorious by default. This is true. Kind of. Not to burst anyone's bubble here, but who wants to be 104 years old when they sell their first novel or see their first credit roll across the silver screen?

THERE ARE BETTER WAYS TO SUCCEED.

First and foremost, become a great writer. Practice. As follows in this book, learn your product and how to market it. That's all practical stuff that will help when the time comes.

But how do you separate yourself from the millions of people out there who call themselves "writers"—enough to populate their own student-loan-impoverished country? How the heck are you planning to leapfrog your way over every other hack with a heartbeat and a word processor?

There are no shortcuts, but some people do have an edge.

Reasons Why an Agent or Editor Will Consider a New Author

1. You've written a salable book. (It could be a hot topic or simply brilliant.)

2. You're a public figure. (Politician, movie star, criminal.)

3. They like you. (Some people are charismatic—if you have it, use it.)

experiences, includ-
writing conference

me, all longing for
d I also found out

4. You're connected. (Your uncle owns a film studio or your best friend is a literary agent.)

5. You have a platform. (Prominent diet doctor, spiritual leader, charity organizer.)

6. You've self-published and sold more than 5,000 copies. (This shows potential.)

There is also a downside to the edge ... anti-edge. With the exception of star players like Stephen King and J.K. Rowling, most writers have to be on their best behavior, be flexible, give it their all, and do it with humility. Not that King and Rowling don't, but when you're that famous, very few people are going to argue with you.

Reasons Why an Agent or Editor Will Dump an Author

1. Life's too short. (Don't complain about money, deadlines, or your husband's medical problems—nobody likes a whiner.)

2. You're a pest. (Don't call or e-mail repeatedly—when they know something, they will contact you.)

3. Missed deadlines. (It costs everyone money.)

4. Intransigence. (If you're asked to make changes, consider them seriously—everyone involved wants a good product.)

5. Criminal behavior/Plagiarism/Lawsuits. (Unless that's what the book is about.)

The previous page is mostly common sense. You need to know how to play the game, and how to play smart. And a warning: Entitlement comes from things acquired too easily. I'm not saying you should suffer for decades. We'll try to skip that. But what you work for, you appreciate more. So earn your success.

experiences, includ-
a writing conference

e me, all longing for
nd I also found out

WE ALL HAVE TO START
SOMEWHERE

Like the start of the universe, things have to come together just right. Books and screenplays do not spontaneously appear. They combust occasionally, but rarely do they form out of nothing. The process of wrestling your writing into existence often requires some of the following: The Idea, Life Experience, and/or Research. These fill the sea with story plankton. When it's ready to evolve and walk on land, it might morph into The Proposal, The Synopsis, The Partial Manuscript, or—the highest level on our evolutionary scale—The Completed Manuscript.

Sounds very academic, doesn't it? Luckily, it's much easier than calculus equations or gene splicing. We'll just take a peek at how a written product develops and what you can do with it along the way.

"Evolution is not a force but a process."
~John Morley

The Idea

The beginning of creative life. This is the point where lightning strikes the nucleic acids in your brain and something starts to move. You cannot copyright an idea. An idea is just that, an idea. Nothing is written down. This doesn't mean that your idea can't be sold for money, but be wary. The great thing about ideas is that they are meant to be developed. They are seeds. If you are careful, they can be shared. Meeting others who are struggling between fantasy and the printed page is a good way to bounce storylines around and decide whether or not this seed of yours should be given life or buried deep. The downside is that there is a chance someone will steal your idea, write the book before you can say "U.S. Copyright Office," and sell it to Hollywood. Years later, you might meander into a theater and see your seed fully grown on the silver screen. The thief will walk the red carpet and collect an Oscar for the dazzling concept that you had first. And it gets worse. The Nobel Prize for literature will be awarded to that no-good writer you blabbed your thoughts to over lunch.

Paranoia runs deep among creative types. Fortunately, there is only a very slim possibility that the above scenario will happen. Even if your idea gets pilfered, it was just an idea. I'd recommend that if cerebral lightning strikes, hustle to a keyboard, pronto.

Life Experience

You've just come from the cruise-ship experience of a lifetime. The massive, fourteen-floor Contessa Guadelupe hit an iceberg. In the Caribbean. The boat sank. And you, thanks to your obsession with sunblock, emptied out your three hundred bottles of Coppertone, tied them together with your pantyhose raft-style, and paddled through shark-infested waters to the safety of Cuba, where you had an affair with Fidel Castro. God almighty, if the TV networks haven't already found you, an agent surely will. While you may not be the first lady or Dianne Fossey, many life experiences are highly marketable to both the book and movie industries.

Life experience can also work on a smaller scale. Maybe your relationships with family, friends, and co-workers have given you great insight into the minds and actions of others. Divorces, deaths, bankruptcies are all fodder for drama. Many teachers advise us to write what we know. This could seriously impair our science-fiction contingent, though using what you know to bring emotional reality to your work, no matter what genre, can also bring success.

Research

San Francisco literary agent Robert Shepard recalls his experience with author and journalist Stefan Fatsis, who wrote the bestseller *Word Freak*. "One of the keys to doing research is to know when to come up for air. It's imperative that an author do as much research as the book needs in order to be accurate and thorough, but not so much that the book is merely cluttered with facts—research for the sake of research alone. Stefan had the luxury of doing a special kind of research involving total immersion in the subject. *Word Freak* is so vivid because he actually lived the experience he recounted, playing in Scrabble tournaments and even sharing hotel rooms with some of the leading players. So the 'research' he did as an author not only rounds out the reader's understanding of the subject and the setting but also moves the narrative forward."

What a fantastic combination of life experience and research. No matter what you write, it's always good to have a thorough understanding of your subject, time period, and character. Many books that involve extensive research, such as *Seabiscuit*, have later sold to Hollywood. Another good example of a well-researched book is *American Nightingale*, a WWII biography of the first nurse killed after the Normandy invasion.

Let's get up onto dry land and paper …

The Proposal

Sound romantic? Trust me, it's not. Prince Charming is not about to ride down from his Hollywood castle, get down on bended knee and offer you a three-picture, multimillion-dollar deal. Nor will the

ious to the telltale
k them as wannabes.

insider know-how
r odds, but without

proposal make an honest writer of you. The proposal is generally used for nonfiction books and documentaries.

THE POINT OF THE PROPOSAL IS TO FIND OUT IF TARGETED PUBLISHING ENTITIES OR NETWORKS FEEL THAT THE BOOK OR DOCUMENTARY IS WORTH DEVELOPING.

It makes sense. Before any serious writing time and funds are committed, it's wise to see if there is a market for *Steam-Powered Street Clocks of America* or *Fetch: A Dog Trainer's Secrets to Successful Non-Canine Relationships*. Many proposals have been sold to publishers on the strength of the outline and a couple of chapters. Ditto for documentaries. Some proposals are viable. Some couldn't get shelf space or airtime on Pluto.

An excellent resource for those wondering if they have what it takes is *Nonfiction Book Proposals Anybody Can Write* by Elizabeth Lyon—a book she sold on the strength of a proposal.

The Synopsis

Depending on what you are writing, a synopsis can be anywhere from a paragraph to a few pages. It's a brief overview of the project you are writing. "I can sometimes get a feel for whether they (the writers) know what they are doing, but really, a synopsis is best for expressing the concept," says Los Angeles literary manager

Colin O'Reilly. He adds, "It depends on genre. A synopsis for drama will be pretty boring, as the reader won't have time to connect with any of the characters. A synopsis is much better suited, in my opinion, to high-concept comedy or sci-fi." A synopsis is used mostly by fiction scribes and screenwriters. It is not required by all agents and is not meant to be a preview of your writing style. Few projects are sold on a synopsis alone.

The Partial Manuscript

Joelle Fraser, author of the award-winning book *The Territory of Men*, can attest to the importance of a good beginning. "In the fall of 1999, my rent check just bounced and I told my agent that I needed to go out with what I had, rather than spend another year trying to write an entire book. She said I would get more money with a whole book. But I needed money." The result? "[After] she helped me shape the eight essays that I had, and also edited my synopses of the eight remaining essays I was proposing, Random House made the offer [of $40,000]. They gave me a year to finish the book."

Where's your $40,000 advance? If you have a partial manuscript of a nonfiction project, and a proposal or synopsis to back up your long-term vision, you may have a winner too.

In fiction, spectacular writing is of interest to the publishing pros, but they will rarely take on an incomplete novel. Especially

ious to the telltale
k them as wannabes.

t insider know-how
r odds, but without

if it is your first. If this is your second, third, or fourth novel, you might have better luck. There are no guarantees.

How about a partial screenplay? Sorry, they're dead in the water. The offices of screen agents are already packed to the rafters with completed scripts that they don't have time to read. There is no reason for them to read anything that isn't finished unless you just came back from a Mars landing or your last name is Spielberg, Lucas, or Coppola.

The Completed Masterpiece

Now you've got product. Whether it's a novel, cookbook, screenplay, article, or memoir, you are in the tiny percentage of writers who actually finished what they began. This is an accomplishment. You deserve the title "writer," though you still need to be able to tell the world what you've got.

y New York
es bestseller
was just an
agent away.
y, somebody
d recognize
my talent,
lling errors
ll. This was
ite the little
ntasy I had
ing between
y ears. I did
ublished …
ntually. But
etting from
reamland to
y, and actu-
y seeing my
me in print,
s an adven-
in discover-
the customs
oreign land
ablishing). I
ned to keep
networking
ar on at all

MANY WRITERS FAIL BECAUSE THEY ARE TRYING TO SELL IN THE WRONG MARKETS

Defining the direction of your manuscript is the all-important first step to presenting yourself as professional. Think of this process as honesty in packaging. Do you want to buy a can of beans, open it, and find asparagus? Neither do the publishing houses. If you've got a can of Chick Lit, such as *Sex and the City*, don't try to feed it to a hungry nonfiction editor. You might not be invited back to dinner.

How will you become an honest writer with a salable product? With accurate descriptions. The big divisions in the book industry are like a map. Instead of North, South, East, and West mixing over four quadrants, we have Fiction, Nonfiction, Literary, and Commercial. Just like the directions, they blend to make Literary Fiction, Commercial Fiction, Literary Nonfiction, and Commercial Nonfiction.

> "Publishing is largely a business of rejection."
>
> ~Angela Rinaldi

Separating Fiction and Nonfiction is pretty easy. Fiction is made up. Nonfiction is real.

Star Wars is fiction. So are most comic books and the movies that follow. Most of the short stories in the *New Yorker* and *Playboy* are fiction. The jury is still out on whether the letters in *Playboy* are fiction or not. Science fiction is obviously fiction even if it comes true later. Jacqueline Susann's *The Valley of the Dolls* is fiction. If it comes from the imagination, it's probably fiction.

A 1996 Corolla car manual is nonfiction. Nonfiction is a presentation of information based on facts, logical speculation, or experience. Eighty percent of all books sold are nonfiction. This book is nonfiction. Biographies, any story based on real events, living people, or historical figures are nonfiction.

There's also creative nonfiction, which is usually based on a history. Remember how dull history class was? Times have changed. While backed up by facts, creative nonfiction combines the author's skill, research, and imagination to breathe life into true events. *I Am Madame X: A Novel* by Gioia Diliberto is a terrific example. Weaving together newspaper accounts of historical events and figures, the story is told from the perspective of Virginie Gautreau, the notorious subject of John Singer Sargent's most famous and scandalous painting.

Also, the witty observations of Dave Barry and Erma Bombeck are nonfiction. Memoirs are nonfiction—and if your

show promise, estab-
don't want younger

ts on their turf. The
closed to you. The

name is Frank McCourt (*Angela's Ashes*), your intense use of language will transcend you to the quadrant of literary nonfiction.

Breaking out Literary and Commercial is a little trickier. Literary (aka drama for screenwriters) stories have a deep, often symbolic meaning. These stories detail fictitious events that have a profound effect on the protagonist or society. Jane Smiley's *A Thousand Acres* is a classic example.

Commercial (sometimes called mainstream) is what the majority of fiction writers write. Built for mass appeal, champions of this market are Stephen King, Dean Koontz, Danielle Steele, Nora Roberts, John Grisham … name all the biggies and chances are they are commercial fiction writers. With success like this, no wonder so many writers want to emulate the heavyweights.

FIELD TRIP

It's time to get out of the house, away from the word processor, and learn, from the real world, where your overall market is.

1. Go to your local bookstore.

2. Picture in your mind an author or book that compares to your work. What book would be next to yours on the shelf?

3. Find it.

4. Look around. What section are you in?

That's your market.

experiences, including a stint as a wr ing conferen coordinator, met thousan of writers ju like me, all longing for their break. And I also found out th there are a series of core truths, truth that writers must learn, accept and overcome if they hope to make it in pu lishing. In fact, these truths apply everywhere and to every-one because the industry a lot like the old high sch cafeteria. Especially to you new kids Unfortunate many writers who strive to make an

A ROSE BY ANY OTHER NAME...
DOESN'T SELL

"If you are going through hell, keep going."

~Sir Winston Churchill

An old fable from India has six blind men touching an elephant and giving their impressions. One holds the tail and calls it a rope. Another cradles the trunk and announces it to be a snake. Yet another, feeling the broad side of the elephant, thinks it's a wall. With the plethora of genres and subgenres, a lot of writers are perplexed and don't know what type of story they've written. So let's get a feel for your elephant.

"Genre is mostly a shorthand way of talking, a way of placing a story within a certain tradition," says Jacquelyn Blain, a producer and writer for hit television series like *Diagnosis Murder* and *Martial Law*. Familiar with the confusion writers face when it comes time to classify what type of story they have, she offers this advice: "What I find is that most people get so caught up in trying to figure out which genre they're writing in that they lose sight of what they're writing. If you've got a dead body or a crime or a puzzle to be solved, you're working in the mystery realm. If you've got an alternative universe of some kind, you're pretty much in science fiction. And then there are all those sub-genres, like cozy and hardboiled, category romance and mainstream romance, suspense and thriller, space opera and fantasy. They're all useful tags because they give the reader a place to start."

Blain admits that too many writers try to play by the rules within each genre and subgenre, figuring that if they don't adhere to those rules, they'll never make a sale. She says, "The truth is that there's room within each genre to do all kinds of interesting, out-of-the-ordinary things. The only genre with real, written-down rules that I know of is category romance, and the individual publishing houses have guidelines available to point a writer in a specific direction if they want to write, say, a Harlequin Intrigue."

You'll find that elements of your project skew more heavily toward one genre than another. Voilà! That's your main genre.

EXCEPT FOR ROMANCE NOVELS AND THE OCCASIONAL DRAMA, LOVE STORIES ARE A SUBPLOT.

ly to you new kids.
many writers who

itors aren't aware of
archies and cutthroat

This requires a pen. Circle all genres that apply to your project.

Action, Adventure, Alien, Animal, Animation, Apocalyptic, Artistic, Biblical, Biographical, Black or Dark, Buddy, Character Driven, Children, Comedy, Coming of Age, Conspiracy, Courtroom, Crime, Detective, Edgy, Environmental, Epic/Saga, Espionage, Family, Fantasy, Farce, Film Noir, Futuristic, Gay/Lesbian, Gen-X, Gritty, High Concept, Holidays, Horror, Love Story, Medical, Murder, Musical, Mystery, Nature, Nonfiction/ History, Occult, Period, Political, Psychopathic, Quirky, Romance, Romantic Comedy, Satire, Sci-Fi, Strong Female Lead (aka Women's Fiction), Supernatural, Surreal, Teen, Terrorist, Thriller, Tragedy, True Story, UFO, Underworld, Urban, War/Military, Western.

*List of genres found at www.inktip.com. In addition, several genres were added by author.

experiences, including a int as a writ- g conference coordinator, I et thousands f writers just like me, all longing for their break. And I also und out that there are a series of core truths, truths that writers must learn, accept and overcome if they hope to ake it in pub- lishing. In fact, these truths apply everywhere and to every- one because e industry is a lot like the old high school cafete- a. Especially to you new kids. nfortunately, many writers who strive to

FICTION WRITERS SUBGENRE
CIRCLE-A-THON

Now see if you can classify your genre further into subgenres.

Anti-culture, Atheistic, Drugs or Alcohol, Ecological, Gangs, Mob, Racial, Immoral Elements, Inspirational, Irreverent, Moral Message, Religious, Spiritual, Molestation/Rape/Incest, Lower Class, Middle Class, High Society, Extreme Sports, Martial Arts, Boxing, Ball Sports, Racing, Winter Sports, Summer Sports, Female Sports, Bodice Ripper, Circus, Contemporary, Disease, Erotica, Fairies, Gambling, Ghost, Glitz, Gothic, Gumshoe, Healing, Interracial, Jazz, Jeopardy, Kidnap, Lost World, Man vs. Industry, Memoir, Nautical, Pirate, Police, Political, Prehistoric, Prison, Prostitution, Refugee, Road Trip, Robbery, Rock and Roll, Slapstick, Slasher, Time Travel, Serial Killer, Sorcery, Spoof, Superhero, Upmarket, Vampire, Trailer Trash Memoir.

(Of course, there are many, many others.)

*List of genres found at www.inktip.com. In addition, several genres were added by author.

fair. It's not. The publishi world is toug to crack. Wh you are in th early stages getting peop to notice you talent, earnir a living through you creative endeavors is like trying t climb Everes with a roll o tooth floss a thumb tacks for spikes. There is no room for am teurs or the equipped. Those alread mining wag from this extremely co petitive indu try don't wa to waste thei time on new comers. And you do show promise, est lished autho don't want younger or

Nonfiction Genres and Subgenres

For you writers in the real world, in *A Writer's Guide to Nonfiction*, Elizabeth Lyon lists the three basic forms of nonfiction:

- articles
- essays
- books

It's pretty easy to figure out which one of the three you're writing. Beyond that she breaks it down again into genres:

- Informational/Educational (Investigative/Exposé, Consumer Product, Consumer Service, Technical)
- How-To (Technical, Self-Help, Inspirational)
- Feature
- Profile (Q&A, Interview)
- Column
- Opinion
- Personal Experience (As Told To, Confession, Inspiration, Nostalgia, Humor, Memoir, Autobiography, Biography/Family History)

And beyond that, writers must consider their style of nonfiction:

- narrative
- practical

- prescriptive
- reference
- pop culture

"The best books within a genre are often ones that push the boundaries in some way, even if they're still working firmly within that genre," says Jacquelyn Blain. Blain cites Diana Gabaldon, who writes noncategory romances, as an example. "Her books combine her genre with time travel, sci-fi and historical fiction. And then there's Alice Hoffman. Pegged as mainstream, she adds a murder mystery to *The River King*, and witches, which are most usually viewed as either horror or fantasy, in *Practical Magic*."

Write down your genre and under it, your subgenres. You now know a lot more about your elephant.

ly to you new kids.
many writers who

itors aren't aware of
archies and cutthroat

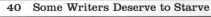

WRITERS ARE LIKE POPCORN:
PUBLISHERS BUY THEM BY THE BUCKET
AND EAT THEM
BY THE HANDFUL

Our views on patriotism, cosmetics, raising children, saving money, and dieting are always changing with current events. Teen angst may spring eternal, but each subsequent generation will express it different-ly. Politics, religion, and spirituality are gold mines that have been worked for decades. The market, for both product and writers, is a living entity. It grows and shrinks as public tastes come and go.

Publishers buy both subjects and writers that they think will sell. As soon as a new fad hits, like a raw-food diet, suddenly a dozen books feature recipes for a raw food lifestyle. If a movie star has a brush with death, or a homeless teenager strums her way to a Grammy Award, bookstore shelves get stocked with tomes that detail their survival and success. In fiction, editors search for genres and

> "First they ignore you, then they laugh at you, then they fight you, then you win."
> ~Mahatma Gandhi

writers that have a proven track record. They seek storylines that fill a void in the marketplace. But their "want" lists change. Constantly.

How will you find your place in the market? By understanding it. "What a writer must possess is knowledge of the industry they wish to become a part of. So many times writers do not feel it is necessary to learn all there is, with respect to the inner workings of the business. This is futile. A writer must know the people, the marketplace, and all of the tools with which he/she will need to stand out over the next guy," says Audrey Kelly, editor-in-chief of *Fade In* magazine.

Sometimes the phenomenal success of a single best-seller can wipe out the market for similar books for years to come. Off the record, one agent told me that ever since *Who Moved My Cheese?* by Spencer Johnson climbed the national sales lists, not a single parable title has sold to New York publishers.

In fiction, the mid-nineties produced a glut of women mystery novelists, as well as *Bridget Jones's Diary*. Author Helen Fielding's runaway success spawned books from hundreds of similar writers who scribbled their way to published novels via cigarettes, alcohol, failed diets, and "singletons." Gluts are good. And bad. When a title or author is hot, publishers are anxious to push similar products and writers into the marketplace. When the boom is over, intense competition develops between writers

r attended a writing
ok signing or literary

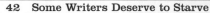

ript, and instead of
event inspired, you

for the few slots publishers have left. Only so many books in a certain area can sell.

Another example of market influence can be seen in the health field. The current requirements for penning a health-related book have become more strict, with publishers demanding that authors have a college degree or verifiable experience in their expertise.

There's more. "Travel memoirs have been done to death," complains one New York editor, citing an overabundance of manuscripts from writers who abandoned professional lives and hit the open road. This is not to say that a travel memoir won't sell, it's just harder to sell one in today's market. A travel memoirist must demonstrate how their unique perspective sets them apart from everyone else. Two good examples in this arena are Peter Mayle's quirky, south of France adventures and Lars Eighner's *Travels With Lizbeth*, a story of a homeless, gay man who traverses the United States with his beloved dog in tow.

Throughout your writing career, you will hear all kinds of pronouncements—like those I've just cited—from editors and agents who have their pulse on the market. Listen carefully, yet accept that the market is in a constant state of flux. It can all change tomorrow.

In the end, you'll have the best chance at publication if you understand the trends (don't blindly follow them), while bringing a fresh perspective to a category you intimately understand.

4 WAYS TO TRACK THE
MARKETPLACE

1. Subscribe to *Publisher's Weekly* ... or at least visit their Web site often.

2. Attend seminars and conferences that host agents, editors, and publishers.

3. Haunt literary Web sites and subscribe to e-newsletters for freelance writers. And the best, cheapest way of all ...

4. Become your librarian's best friend.

To elaborate on No. 4, you can at least become her best and friendliest customer. My local librarian knows I write. When she's buying new books she keeps me in mind as she reads through the lists of all the recently released titles. Hello! Can you say "research assistant"? For free! Books are these people's lives. They are walking universities on the marketplace, and it's not hard to draw them out of their paper shells.

feel like you are on the ou side looking at your successful, published friend and acquain tances? Have you ever attended a writing conf ence, book signing or li erary gather ing knowing that you hav a great man script, and instead of le ing the even inspired, yo wind up feel ing intimida ed by the se ingly insurmountable w of people wh are already i the game? It doesn't seem fair. It's not. The publishi world is tou, to crack. Wl you are in tl early stages getting peor

NEPOTISM HAPPENS

"Luke, I am your father."
~Darth Vader

Most of us have the same problem. With family, friends, acquaintances, and charismatic people at parties, the line ahead of us to get a professional's attention is pretty long. Short of sending yourself off to an orphanage and luckily being adopted by a nice couple with the last name of Murdoch, Bertelsmann, or Pearson, we publishing kingdom commoners must find ways around the beast called Nepotism.

Unless, of course, you can use it to your advantage. True nepotism is about family. Business nepotism is about common ground. The closer, the better. There are six levels of separation.

1. Blood

2. Marriage

3. Friendship

4. Acquaintance

5. Friend of a friend

6. Common interest

One through five are pretty easy to use. You pick up the telephone, introduce yourself, and state your relationship. Number six takes more work. Research.

When you have selected the people you wish to contact, look them up on the Internet. Google them. Look for anything you both have in common. Charities, hobbies, schools, residences, favorite vacation spots, pet peeves, political standing, condiments that should or should not be placed on a hamburger. Find something.

In a single letter or e-mail, state your common ground and make a request. It may be for advice (a clever start to building a relationship), or that you wish them to review your work. Remember, I said a single letter or e-mail. Multiple queries may result in a restraining order.

Another way to use business nepotism is to get social. The more people you know, the more people you can pressure into introducing you to their acquaintances. Just don't press too hard or too blatantly. This often results in the opposite effect that you desire.

If you're not a social animal, but a hard worker, consider an internship with your targeted company. Age isn't always a factor. Just last year I met a retired writer in his sixties interning at a

g world is tough to
you are in the early

earning a living
creative endeavors is

company. He made connections and later a sale there. It doesn't always work, but at least you will be meeting people in the business.

Why is nepotism so revolting and alluring? Well, the draw is that it's easy. It's the fast track. What most people don't take into account is that to succeed, the Nepotee is still required to work hard and show their talent. The idiot son of the publisher won't be allowed inside for long. All of us must prove our literary worth.

Nepotistic Checklist

1. Check the family tree—is there anyone remotely connected to the business?
2. Check with your friends, your family's friends, your friends' friends—does anyone know someone?
3. Expand to acquaintances.
4. Check social organizations for contacts—churches, charities, purebred dog societies, Masons, VFWs, outreach programs, museum openings, schools, and rehab clinics.
5. Find a good reason to be where the industry people are—get a job, intern, deliver bottled water.

for jobs and contacts on their turf. The door remains closed to you. The process of finding someone, other than your mother, who will champion your book takes on the surreal feeling of a high school cafete-

ly New York
es bestseller
was just an
agent away.
ly, somebody
ld recognize
my talent,
elling errors
all. This was
ite the little
antasy I had
ing between
y ears. I did
published…
entually. But
getting from
reamland to
ty, and actu-
ly seeing my
me in print,
as an adven-
in discover-
the customs
foreign land
ublishing). I
rned to keep
networking
dar on at all

48   Some Writers Deserve to Starve

MOST PUBLISHERS WILL NOT CONSIDER
A MANUSCRIPT TWICE

"You've got to be careful if you don't know where you're going, because you might not get there."

~Yogi Berra

The Big Six have you under surveillance.

The mere mention of "corporate merger" can make agents and editors shudder. Words like "downsizing" and "outsourcing" have a similar effect. Over the last two decades, while thousands of independent publishers emerged, the major houses have undergone shift after shift as giant corporations swallow up each other and any successful independent publishers in their path.

The result? If you're a writer, editor, agent, manager, or producer, this means there are fewer buyers of content than ever before. The vast majority of all printed and broadcast product comes from six mega-conglomerates. Who are they? What companies do they own?

- Pearson (Penguin, Putnam, Viking, Dutton, Puffin, New American Library, Signet, Plume, and others)

- Bertelsmann (Random House, Knopf, Anchor, Bantam, Doubleday, Vintage, Crown, and others)

- TimeWarner (Warner Books, DC Comics, Time, Inc., HBO, AOL, and many others)

- Holtzbrinck (St. Martin's Press, Macmillan, Picador, Farrar, Straus & Giroux, and others)

- Murdoch's News Corporation (20th Century Fox, Fox, HarperCollins, and many others)

- Viacom (Simon & Schuster, Pocket Books, CBS, Paramount, Showtime, BET, MTV, and others)

For writers, the bad news doesn't stop at limited content. These behemoths took a cue from the FBI and now use computer databases to store information on submitted manuscripts (title, author, and any other pertinent info). Ditto for studios and screenplays. If you've submitted material, congratulations, you have a record! If the work is rejected, guess what? That rejection is on file with all the companies under the conglomerate's roof. And few editors will look at a manuscript again.

Yet writers still submit material on their own all the time. Sometimes editors invite writing conference attendees to send in work, sometimes a query letter will spark their interest, and occa-

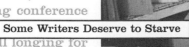

experiences, includ-
a writing conference

e me, all longing for
nd I also found out

sionally a writer will send an unsolicited manuscript that gets read. Just be aware that if you send work to them, and they reject it, you've damaged your chances of publishing that project, with that house, in the future.

Is it hopeless? No. Some editors who have formed strong ties with certain agents will give an author a second chance. But don't count on it. Once an agent discovers that a writer has submitted material to all the major houses, there is little chance that they'll take that author on.

Isn't there a way to fool them? You could reset the margins, change the page count, rename the characters, and make up a new title. It's been done many times. The problem: there is a summary of your work. And trying to put one over on them pisses off editors. Wouldn't you rather take your rejection with your head held high and the knowledge that you can submit your next project?

Fortunately, there is some good news. If you submit without an agent, and an editor at one of the Big Six LOVES your work and wants to buy it, you'll often be told to get an agent for your own protection. This makes finding an agent a cinch.

Presentation Is Everything: Manuscript Etiquette
Here are a few tips and tricks to keep your manuscript from immediately landing in the rejection pile.

- Don't put copyright warnings or WGA registration numbers on your work. Keep it simple.

- Anything other than your work and a brief note thanking the editor or agent for requesting your material is taboo. That means no photos, no coverage, no artwork—no matter how enticing the additions might be.

- Plays list a cast of characters at the beginning. Feature film scripts and books do not.

- Never send out your manuscript in a three-ring binder. Stretch a rubber band around it. No three-hole-punch paper unless it's a screenplay—and they have their own rules. Use plain white paper, though brightness (level of white) counts.

- Buy a good printer or have decent quality copies made.

- No color paper or colored inks. Ever. Black text on white paper. Only.

- If you print it yourself: Use quality paper. If possible, a new ink cartridge. Clear, crisp letters vs. the splatter effect of the refilled-too-many-times ink cartridge makes your work easier to read.

- The ink on professionally photocopied pages doesn't run.

- If your work is returned to you, never send the used manuscript or screenplay out a second time—even if it looks barely read. Recycle it to family, friends, or the environment.

experiences, includ-
a writing conference

ke me, all longing for
nd I also found out

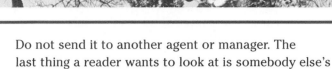

Do not send it to another agent or manager. The last thing a reader wants to look at is somebody else's thumbprint or coffee ring.

Printer Wisdom

I love Hollywood. Movies and television that portray writers seldom, if ever, show the nitty-gritty side of producing the product. Sure, Carrie Bradshaw might peck out a few words here and there, but who's ever seen a printer in her New York apartment? Who has ever witnessed any printer in any as-seen-on-TV writer's abode?

My point? The printer is an integral part of our writing process. We might imagine ourselves editing novels and screenplays right off our computer monitors (and saving a few trees in the process), yet the reality of any working writer's life is that we need physical evidence of our labors. Even if it's just for self-editing purposes. Thus, the printer.

The downside of writing and printing is that it gets expensive. Paper and ink cartridges add up, then add in the cost of a decent quality printer … suddenly the financial reality of our work is that we are spending hundreds of dollars per year, if not more, on printing. And not all of us are at a point where we can write these costs off on our taxes.

When you're starting out, it's often important to save a few bucks—especially if you've foregone a traditional lifestyle, quit your day job, and decided that come hell or high water you're going to become a professional writer, no matter what.

That said, take a few tips from the word mines …

1. Learn to refill your ink cartridges. You'll save hundreds of dollars per year. Practice makes perfect, so don't expect to be the Michelangelo of ink cartridge refillers right off the bat. Follow all directions at first, then, after you find a system or refill product that works for you, stock up.

2. When I was writing my first novel, I was horrified by the amount of paper I used to print out drafts—drafts that usually wound up in the recycle bin. Even though I was buying paper by the box, I was still burning through paper at a cost of about $50 per month. The solution? I cut my costs in half by using both sides of the page. If it was a rough draft that was going to be tossed anyway, I simply drew a line through the "used" pages, flipped them over and printed new drafts on the blank side.

    Eventually, as one of my New Year's resolutions, I stopped this practice. It was at this time that my writing had improved drastically and I wasn't using as much paper.

3. There's a time to be cheap and a time to spend a few extra bucks. Double-sided drafts don't leave your possession unless it's in the aforementioned recycle bin. Material printed

experiences, includ-
a writing conference

e me, all longing for
nd I also found out

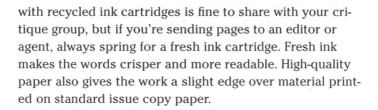

with recycled ink cartridges is fine to share with your critique group, but if you're sending pages to an editor or agent, always spring for a fresh ink cartridge. Fresh ink makes the words crisper and more readable. High-quality paper also gives the work a slight edge over material printed on standard issue copy paper.

truths that writers must learn, accept and overcome
if they hope to make it in publishing. In fact, these
truths apply everywhere and to everyone because the
industry is a lot like the old high school cafeteria.

is was quite
ittle fantasy
had playing
en my ears.
did get pub-
d...eventual-
But getting
a dreamland
reality, and
ually seeing
my name in
rint, was an
ture in dis-
ing the cus-
of a foreign
nd (publish-
I learned to
eep my net-
rking radar
at all times
never know
vho you will
t) and, most
all, face the
fact that the
ntain I was
ing to climb
vas nothing

ALL PUBLISHERS ARE
NOT CREATED
EQUAL

In the beginning, during the Paleolithic era of publishing, when writers chiseled out their magnum opuses on stone tablets ... okay, maybe not that far back. A long time ago, decades ago, writers would write their tomes, lick a stamp, cross their fingers, and mail their work off to the brand-name publishers in Manhattan. According to the myth still perpetuated in Hollywood movies today, sophisticated, ascot-wearing, martini-swilling editors await these masterpieces. They eagerly rip open the envelopes containing these unsolicited manuscripts, seize upon the brilliance within and declare it a sure-fire best-seller. Some myths need to be bulldozed like Schwab's drugstore on the Sunset Strip.

Unless you have an agent, the Big Six media conglomerates, who own most of the brand-name pub-

"When choosing between two evils, I always like to try the one I've never tried before."
~Mae West

lishing enterprises, are closed to you. Is that the end of your infant publishing career? Does no agent equal no access? No.

Fortunately, not all publishers are created equal. While many New York-based publishers are equipped with warning labels and Web pages trumpeting the fact that they do not accept unsolicited anything of any kind, smaller and alternative publishers have a different take on submissions. Many do not require you to be represented by an agent.

Your options include privately owned publishers, university presses, print-on-demand publishers, e-publishers, downloadable books, and self-publishing.

Privately Owned Publishers

There are thousands of privately owned publishers in North America, Europe, and all over the globe. They range from companies that print a few dozen titles a year, like Multnomah Publishers in Sisters, Oregon, that published the best-selling *Prayer of Jabez*, to companies like Chronicle Books with approximately 175 books published annually. Geography doesn't matter. If you have what they are looking for, these publishers could be your ticket to success.

How will you know if one of these publishers is a match for your book? Like I said, there are thousands of independent publishers. So start online. An excellent place to begin is "Preditors & Editors," a site that offers reviews of agents and publishers.

el like you are on the
g in at your success-

you ever attended a
ence, book signing or

It can be found at www.anotherealm.com/prededitors. From there, link to the hundreds of publisher Web sites and review their policies. Submission guidelines are rarely on the home page, so look for pull-down menus with words and phrases such as "about us," "contact us," "guidelines," "submissions," and "query and manuscript submissions."

University Presses

University presses seek scholarly efforts, in many cases ones that have a connection to their region. Each university has a specific publishing program. While some look for historical efforts, others smile upon medical or literary efforts. Much like the independent publishers, the best way to discover whether or not you've got the manuscript for them is to examine their submission guidelines posted on university Web sites. A great resource for research is the Association of American University Presses (www.aaupnet.org).

Print-on-Demand

Is print-on-demand (POD) publishing purgatory or a legitimate venture? This is an area of publishing that's still defining itself. Authors are paid only for the copies of their book that sell. That's because the book is stored electronically, in the company's system, until someone buys it. Books are produced one copy, one request at a time.

Some POD publishers have no upfront fees and no minimum number of books to buy after publication, but promotion is left to the author. You have to push it to the bookstores. You have to get it reviewed in the media. You have to push, pull, and drag your book into the public awareness. If you don't have a lot of money, but have plenty of time and a knack for self-promotion, this can be an effective method.

Some POD publishers, such as iUniverse, Xlibris, and AuthorHouse, are fee-charging. The author pays a one-time setup fee, then receives royalties on copies sold. Many of these companies offer promotional packages to help you announce your book to the world. If you are considering a publicity package, find out what you're getting before you commit.

There are some fantastic success stories concerning POD authors getting their books optioned for movies and catching the attention of big-name literary agents. Yet print-on-demand books have yet to hit the best-seller lists or be fully accepted in the traditional publishing community. The reason for this has to do with distribution. At the time of this printing, most products from POD publishers are not distributed through mainstream channels (like Ingram or Partners/West that supply books to chain stores and independent sellers), and that means there is no return policy on unsold books. Unsold inventory ties up a bookseller's cash flow—unless of course they can return it for

el like you are on the
g in at your success-

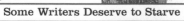

you ever attended a
ence, book signing or

a credit and buy the next up-and-coming hot title that they hope to turn a profit on.

The POD route requires the writer to think like a businessman, not a creative type. In 2002, I used PublishAmerica for my first novel, *Zeus & His Mighty Nine Iron*. There was no cost to me, and overall, I was pleased with the quality of the printing and cover art. The advance against future sales was one dollar, and my experience with this publisher has been a good one so far. Through a lot of promotion on my part, the book sold well regionally and is now carried in select Barnes & Noble stores, as well as several independent booksellers. It's also offered online, but to be honest, there have been few sales via the Internet.

I chose PublishAmerica because I had exhausted all other avenues. Kind of. The same day PublishAmerica offered me a publishing contract, I was independently offered the chance to work with a New York literary agent who wanted me to do a major rewrite of Zeus. At that point, I had been working on the novel for two years. I wanted out. I wanted the book off my desk. I wanted to move on. Who knows what would have happened if I had accepted the agent's offer. There were no guarantees of success either way. One side held the possibility of having a rewritten novel sold to one of the Big Six, the other, a guaranteed book in my hands and on my shelf in six months.

If you're considering a print-on-demand publisher, return to www.anotherealm.com/prededitors, the "Preditors & Editors" page of publishers. I hope that you will do a considerable amount of research before you commit your time and/or money to this process. Link over to the home pages of the POD publishers that catch your interest. Study the submission guidelines. Read the publishing contract carefully. You'll quickly find out which companies are fronts for editing services and which ones produce quality authors and products.

E-Publishing

E-publishing is still relatively new. E-books can be downloaded into a personal digital assistant or read off a computer screen. Many e-publishers operate just like traditional publishing houses, except they don't offer advances and have higher royalty rates. Companies like AuthorHouse, who e-published Amanda Brown's *Legally Blonde*, offer authors the opportunity to get in print … fast. The fees vary. Some offer editing, formatting, and media services in addition to an upfront e-publishing charge. Others offer a one-time membership buy-in (like timeshares) and up to 75 percent royalties after that, depending on the contract you sign. On the subject of contracts, be very careful about what you sign. Read every word and if you don't understand something, find or hire someone who does. Also check out the official organization for e-publishing at www.epicauthors.com, for a list of legitimate publishers.

el like you are on the
g in at your success-

you ever attended a
ence, book signing or

INTERNATIONAL

Downloadable Books

Downloadable books are similar to e-publishing, but readers purchase the product directly from the author's Web site and either print a copy of the book or read the information off their computer. To me, this is the most exciting area of publishing. It's an area that constantly redefines itself as it grows by leaps and bounds.

After writing a book on bipolar disorder, then having it ignored by the agent who had requested it, author Julie Fast launched her Web site, www.bipolarhappens.com, in May 2002. The book was available only to download. She made her first sale on launch day and another $3,000 worth of sales in the month that followed. Two months later she had a book contract with New Harbinger Publications, and later that year a literary agent sought Fast out and made a second sale for her to Penguin. In the meantime, her downloadable books continue to sell an average of $8,000 per month. But downloadable books aren't the no-brainer you might think. Even with search-engine optimizing, the huge problem with these books is advertising. It costs money to make money. Fast estimates one-third of her online income is spent on advertising.

Is selling your book online a viable option? Maybe. Nonfiction is a natural for information-seeking Web surfers, but the most popular titles aren't dry, academic offerings. Instead, they're written in an engaging, conversational style that hooks the reader right from the very first click of her mouse.

Self-Publishing

Self-publishing requires the author to wear many hats. Editor. Cover designer. Publicity person. Distributor. And guess who foots the bill, too? The author.

So why would you choose this route if you've found a POD willing to cover the initial costs of publishing your book? Think of this as a big gamble. The POD places a bet on your book, figuring that you'll sell enough copies to cover their investment. But if your book is a huge success, guess who keeps most of the money? Guess who gets the lion's share of any movie option bucks? Yes, the POD. They took the risk; they keep the cash. On the other hand, companies that charge authors up-front fees don't have as much invested. Their emphasis is on making a saleable product, not necessarily sales.

After your initial investment to self-publish your book (with or without a vanity press to assist you), you own the books. You own the rights (read the contract to make sure you own the rights). If you can sell the books or the rights, you turn a profit.

Craig Danner, the author of the self-published book *Himalayan Dhaba*, a book that went on to sell reprint rights for a six-figure sum, knows the game. "To succeed, a self-published book needs to exceed expectations. It has to look, feel, and read as if it was the favorite project of a senior editor at a big publisher. Anything

el like you are on the
g in at your success-

you ever attended a
nce, book signing or

less, and it's just another vanity publication, and there are too many good books to bother reading a dud."

Dave Chilton originally self-published *The Wealthy Barber*, a book that went on to sell two million copies. Distributed through black-owned salons and bookstores, E. Lynn Harris's self-published *Invisible Life* sold over 10,000 copies, piquing the interest of New York publishers. Kenn Harper self-published *Give Me My Father's Body*. He sold copies at his store on Baffin Island. A lot of copies. The rest, as they say, is history. It wasn't long before Harper had a deal with a major house and Hollywood knocking at his door.

The percentage of self-published stories that have a dream-come-true ending are small, but they do happen. There can also be drawbacks … like having a garage full of books collecting dust.

Most authors don't self-publish until they've exhausted all other means of getting their work into print. But if you believe your book will have mass appeal, you hone your craft to professional standards, and you have the drive to push your vision on the public, this may be the way for you. And there are exceptions to this self-published-writer-against-the-world image. Ernest Hemingway, Beatrix Potter, Edgar Rice Burroughs, and Deepak Chopra have all self-published. They put up the money. They kept the profits.

A PRO LIST
OF THE BIG SIX &
ALTERNATIVE PUBLISHERS

If your book isn't picked up by the Big Six, are you a failure? No! Other presses have a lot to offer.

Big Six Pros
- National distribution
- Advances ($$$)
- Access to the company publicist

Independent Publisher Pros
- Open to edgier work
- Often develop close relationships with authors and offer more editorial care
- Some titles stay in print longer ... which equals more royalties

University Press Pros
- Prestige
- Often publish titles with a regional appeal
- Speaking/teaching possibilities

feel like you are on the ou side looking at your successful, published friend and acquaintances? Have you ever attended a writing confe ence, book signing or lit erary gather ing knowing that you hav a great manu script, and instead of lea ing the event inspired, you wind up feeling intimidat ed by the see ingly insurmountable w of people who are already in the game? It doesn't seem fair. It's not. The publishi world is toug to crack. Wh you are in th early stages getting peopl

in the early stages of getting people to tice your talnt, earning a ving through your creative endeavors is like trying to climb Everest with a roll of oth floss and thumb tacks for spikes. There is no oom for amaurs or the ill equipped. Those already ining wages from this extremely competitive industry don't vant to waste their time on newcomers. And if you do now promise, established authors don't vant younger more talented scribes ying for jobs and contacts on their turf.

Print-on-Demand Publishers Pros
- Books are in print quickly
- More author control in editing
- Books available online

E-Publishing Pro:
- Public has quick access to your work

Downloadable Publishing Pro
- Instant availability equals instant income

Self-Publishing Pros
- Unlimited potential
- Complete control
- Some of the greatest writers in history have self-published

A CON LIST
OF THE BIG SIX &
ALTERNATIVE PUBLISHERS

Big Six Cons

- That publicist may have 141 other newly launched titles to promote besides yours.
- Just because you make a sale with a big publisher doesn't guarantee a published book. If sales & marketing don't receive enough pre-orders of your title, they may cut losses and cancel your book before it goes to print.

Independent Publisher Cons

- Small to moderate advances
- Limited publicity (author is required to do a lot of marketing)

University Press Cons

- Limited distribution
- Small to moderate advances

Print-On-Demand Publisher Cons

- Limited distribution outside the Internet

feel like you are on the ou side looking at your successful, published friend and acquaintances? Have you ever attended a writing confe ence, book signing or lit erary gather ing knowing that you have a great manu script, and instead of lea ing the event inspired, you wind up feel ing intimidat ed by the see ingly insur mountable w of people wh are already i the game? It doesn't seem fair. It's not. The publishi world is toug to crack. Wh you are in th early stages getting peopl

- Author is responsible for publicity
- Possibility of editing errors
- Low, if any, advance
- Not accepted in mainstream publishing communities (less prestige)
- Most PODs charge fees

E-Publishing Cons
- Limited to online distribution
- Some e-publishers charge fees
- At the time of this printing, e-publishing is still a relatively new concept

Downloadable Publishing Cons
- Set-up costs and promotional overhead
- Suited to nonfiction (fiction has yet to find its market in this arena)

Self-Publishing Cons
- Cost
- Self-distribution can limit sales
- Sales and promotion are entirely your responsibility

want to look for an easier occupation like nuclear
astrophysics or Olympic water polo. Remember, this
isn't a book on how to write, why to write, or what to

you are in
early stages
tting people
notice your
, earning a
ng through
ur creative
vors is like
ng to climb
erest with a
tooth floss
humb tacks
ikes. There
no room for
teurs or the
ll equipped.
ose already
ning wages
from this
emely com-
ve industry
n't want to
their time
newcomers.
d if you do
w promise,
established
thors don't

SOMETIMES THE POT OF GOLD AT THE END OF THE RAINBOW
DOESN'T HOLD MUCH GOLD

First, let's look at the bright side. I don't believe that Stephen King is out mowing lawns to supplement his income. Many authors make a very nice living from their creative endeavors.

Now the bad news: most don't. Thousands of published authors must keep their day jobs or find other streams of revenue. These streams may include teaching classes, editing, manuscript consultation, and judging contests.

For the novice writer, this can be good news. Many well-versed, experienced authors are available to help you … for a price. Just remember when paying them that you may be glimpsing your own future.

In the time of B.P. (Before Publication), you know you will be struggling, working a day job (or living off the kindness of loved ones), hunting contacts, study-

"I'm living so far beyond my income that we may almost be said to be living apart."

~e. e. cummings

ing the business, and basically holding your nose to the grindstone day in and day out. So when the gates open on your publishing dream and your book comes forth onto the hallowed shelves of the booksellers, doesn't everything change? I wish.

There are two main career killers in our business: burnout and the vacuum. Burnout destroys the more seasoned writers while the vacuum thins the numbers of the newly published.

Burnout

This is pretty simple. The writer gets tired. Nothing feels fresh. The word "hack" keeps popping into the writer's mind.

HOW TO AVOID BURNOUT:
1. HAVE A LIFE
2. HAVE A LIFE
3. HAVE A LIFE

Having a life—to me—translates as read, talk with friends, go places (near and far), do things, feel things, and sometimes you just have to put the writing away for awhile.

The Vacuum

In vacuum-afflicted writers, this is the emptiness that follows a first sale. Some call it the curse of the three-book deal. Many writers

eling. All too well. I
of those writing con-

ig and manuscript
y chest, I lined up

focus on their project exclusively for so many years that once it is out, there is nothing left. I interviewed a former best-selling author whose breakthrough first novel (you'd recognize the title instantly) was lauded by *The New York Times*, won armloads of awards, was translated into over a dozen languages, became a *Reader's Digest* condensed book, and was optioned by Hollywood producers. The publisher celebrated the author's success and flew him to New York for a party thrown in his honor.

When the fanfare subsided, and he sat down at his computer to fulfill his three-book contract, he didn't have the foggiest clue what he was going to write. Sadly, his second novel suffered from weak sales. His third effort was rejected altogether. And his fourth, a memoir of sorts, has not even sparked the interest of his agent. Fortunately, the author, a practical man with a life outside of publishing and bills to pay, knew it was time to return to work.

How to Avoid the Vacuum

1. Keep a creative file. Fill it with story ideas. Interesting characters. Snippets of dialog.

2. Bring a co-writer onboard.

3. Start now! That's right, before your first book is even sold. You have pens. You have paper. It's the perfect time to outline those next books.

"It's a tough, tough business," says one full-time author. Unable to meet her monthly expenses, she confessed that the advance for her next book would not be enough for her to catch up financially.

Are you ready for the writer's life? Is it worth it? Well, it is for me and thousands like me. I love seeing my name in print. I love sharing my thoughts through my words. It's definitely worth the risk and tribulations. And, by the way, do you need someone to mow your lawn?

eling. All too well. I
f those writing con-

ig and manuscript
y chest, I lined up

THERE ARE A LOT OF TEACHERS
WHO SHOULDN'T BE TEACHING

Throw a rock and you will probably hit a writing class. There is an abundance. From MFA programs at prestigious film academies to one-day workshops that roam the globe, it's easy to toss your money in a hundred different directions. Monster bucks are at stake: You shell them out and the teachers rake them in.

The majority of instructors who offer their two cents do so with good intentions. Some even have a passion for sharing their knowledge. Nothing makes them more proud than inspiring others to great works and seeing hungry minds blossom under their guidance.

And then there are the quick-buck artists. Nothing will derail your dreams faster than falling prey to teachers who pump up their audience with

"There's many a best-seller that could have been prevented by a good teacher."
~Flannery O'Connor

false promises (like writing a manuscript or screenplay in as little as a few weeks) then drain their cash reserves. That said, education is part of your journey to turning pro. Making wise classroom choices is up to you … as is avoiding the less-than-honest pseudo-instructors.

The Author-a-saurus

Rumors of their extinction have been greatly exaggerated. Experience is a great teacher. Better if that experience is yours. Many older writers (film scribes, movie-of-the-week mavens, once-famous authors) become excellent teachers and mentors. There are also many who, when their talents flag, hit the seminar circuit to reminisce. The Author-a-saurus extols the exploits of bygone eras. We would hope that if Aristotle were still around today, he'd be lecturing on the three-act structure, NOT waxing poetic about his first big break in ancient Greece and how he nailed that posh philosophy gig.

The Magician

Their slick road shows have you slap down your credit card faster than they can recite the list of celebrities who have supposedly been inspired by their teachings. Hollywood sharks, with cobweb-strewn credits, promise to have you on the inside track by the end of the weekend. These Magicians have been "pitching" their

experiences, includ-
a writing conference

e me, all longing for
nd I also found out

whole lives, and now, abracadabra, they've focused their talents on you … or more precisely, your wallet. By the time you finish reading the "alakazam" cue card, the Magician has split town and your money has vanished.

The Fortune-Teller

They lure you in with incredible offers, give you a taste of your incredible future for just a few dollars, then before you know it, incredibly, you're hanging on their every word. Talent, fame, and fortune are all in your prose, but … whoops … the meter just ran out. Pay up if you want to hear more. These creative seers offer ongoing classes. Their hook is selling novice writers high praise and visions of success. If your faith in their predictions waver, and you don't sign up for the next set of expensive sessions, they tell you that without their special guidance you are doomed to fail.

Mr. & Mrs. Happy-Happy-Nice

Some teachers refuse to confront reality. They stand in front of their class and smile. Smile hard. Really hard. They live in a place called "Happy-Happy-Nice-Land." When confronted with the gruesome truth of just how tough it is to break into the publishing or movie business, they gloss over facts and proclaim "everybody can be a star." Think of these teachers as your dysfunctional parents—post-nervous breakdown. Should you take their class?

Absolutely! They might be one volume short of an encyclopedia set, but they are often whizzes at teaching craft. If you run across one of these types, smile kindly at them and remind yourself that it takes a lot of medication to keep them functioning at their current level of optimism.

The War Hero

The flip side of Happy-Happy-Nice is the grizzled pro. Since this industry churns and burns writers and execs at an astounding rate, there are thousands of loudmouths out there who are only too happy to share war stories of getting books published and movies made. Should you go to their classes or order their books through the local library? By all means, yes! This is an excellent opportunity to learn what it takes to get your vision in print or on the silver screen. However, the War Hero is a fabulously charismatic personality. Don't become a groupie.

The Conference Junkie

These minor-league pros make a meager living jetting from writing conference to writing conference pretending to be a big shot. Conference Junkies are scurrilous so-called professionals that talk a good game, but have few, if any credits. When cornered and asked to produce credits, they offer obscure, often unverifiable references, and spout some terrific lines about how tough the

experiences, includ-
a writing conference

e me, all longing for
nd I also found out

industry has been lately (while it is tough, real agents, editors, and authors still make real sales). For Conference Junkies, writing conferences are a welcome respite from their daily lives. Where else can they be chauffeured, pampered, have their ass kissed, and still turn a few bucks from teaching a class or two? These people aren't dangerous, and you might even learn a thing or two, but for heaven's sake don't take them seriously, don't pick up their restaurant tab, don't get suckered into buying their critique services, and, most of all, don't lend them any money—not even for cab fare to the airport.

Choose the Right Class

1. Know what type of writing you are interested in. If you don't know, or have several areas you would like to explore, experiment. Low-cost classes at a community college or other venue will help you develop your direction.

2. Before you sign up for that MFA writing degree, ask yourself what you think it will do for you. Be honest. Having a writing degree might qualify you to work or teach in a number of writing-related fields, but it won't convince a literary agent to read your manuscript. Talent will.

3. When you know what you want to write, focus on that. If you're a slow-writing sci-fi novelist, don't force yourself into a screenwriting class because you think you can skim

a couple hundred pages off your finished product. Writing a script is just as hard as writing a novel.

4. Similarly, don't be suckered into taking a class because "this opportunity might not be offered again." Unless the old Author-a-saurus is dying, chances are the class will come around again. And again. Select a class that's right for you right now.

5. Beware of classes taught by agents who offer possible representation. They may guarantee that they'll read your script, but don't expect this Magician to call back unless they are offering another class in your area.

6. Watch out for hidden costs. Weekend seminars are famous for getting you in the door with a low-cost offer then hyping the books/tapes/videos/CDs that you must have (usually self-distributed products that are not available in national retail chains). If you don't whip out the credit card, you risk being ignored by the instructor all weekend. If you do, it'll be an expensive way to learn.

7. Try before you buy. Use your local library. Check out books on writing craft. It's FREE and a lot can be learned from studying.

8. Legit instructors do not charge for introductions to industry pros. Creative charlatans will tell you that when your

experiences, includ-
a writing conference

e me, all longing for
nd I also found out

project is "ready," they will allow you to purchase their hard-won contacts. Maybe even throw in a recommendation or two. Of course, this is a ruse. It could be years, if ever, before these Fortune-Tellers deem your work "ready."

9. When the ad for the class touts more celebrity names than actual content, run. Far away. This is the mark of a Magician.

10. Not satisfied? Honest instructors and learning institutions offer refunds for the unused portion of your classes. Usually there is a cutoff period. Ask in advance if you have this option.

11. Never pay more than you can afford. If post-secondary degrees, classes, courses, sessions, weekend workshops, or conferences cause you or your family members financial hardship, consider not signing up. If you must go, see if they need volunteers, offer a trade of services (great if you're a mechanic), or pull a *Good Will Hunting* and take a janitor position at the college.

12. If it's too good to be true … you know the adage. Classes and schools that make big promises seldom deliver. Jobs, agents, and completed projects are almost never realized when the student graduates from these weekend and multi-week courses. Writing craft takes years, not weeks, to develop.

THE TEN RULES OF
THE CLASSROOM

1. If you arrive late, do not expect the teacher to backtrack for your benefit. If you missed out on important information, ask another student during a break or approach the teacher after the class.

2. Never interrupt a teacher. Put your hand up to ask a question. Ask when you are called upon.

3. Never insist that you know more than the instructor. You don't. Even if you have an example of a different way of doing things, or information contrary to what the instructor is saying, keep it to yourself.

4. Don't introduce yourself or give your personal history before you ask your question.

5. Never couch your question with a pitch for your project. Instructors see right through this ploy. At best, they will be annoyed with you. At worst, they will cut you off midsentence.

6. If another instructor has a different way of doing things, don't pop your hand in the air and exclaim, "But Joseph Campbell said ..." It's a big world out there. One that accommodates many different opinions on a myriad of subjects and techniques.

n't seem fair. It's not. The publishing world is toug to crack. Wh you are in th early stages getting peop to notice you talent, earnir a living through you creative endeavors is like trying to climb Everes with a roll of tooth floss ar thumb tacks for spikes. There is no room for ama teurs or the equipped. Those alread mining wage from this extremely co petitive indu try don't war to waste thei time on new-comers. And you do show promise, esta lished author don't want

7. "I loved how you nailed the emotion in the third scene of the second act of your book/ movie because …" Never blather on about the instructor's credits before asking your question. They know them already. So does the rest of the class.

8. Keep your questions short. Get to your point. Be brief. Asking questions in reference to how it relates to your writing is fine. Dwelling on how it relates to your project is not. Furthermore, giving examples as to how the instructor's advice won't work for you will not make you popular with the teacher or your fellow students. So try to ask questions for the good of the class.

9. Ask a question. Get an answer. If you don't like the answer, don't use it.

10. If you feel your project is so unique that it defies all technique, all craft in the history of the written word … classes may not be right for you. Insisting that you wrote your book in "episodes" (vs. chapters or other traditional means) will not win you any points. Don't get fancy. Don't tell the teacher your work is "special" or that "chapters are for common writers." Writing is writing is writing. You either know what you are doing on the page or you are there to learn.

York Times
stseller was
st an agent
way. Surely,
body would
nize my tal-
nt, spelling
ors and all.
is was quite
ittle fantasy
had playing
en my ears.
did get pub-
d...eventual-
But getting
dreamland
reality, and
ually seeing
my name in
rint, was an
ture in dis-
ing the cus-
of a foreign
nd (publish-
I learned to
eep my net-
rking radar
at all times

TRUTH #12

WRITERS RARELY HELP
OTHER
WRITERS

I had always assumed that writers were like a fraternity; once you join, you are brothers in arms for life. In critique groups, local writer organizations, and conferences, there is a reassuring facade of camaraderie. Competition lurks under that facade.

In a perfect world, we would all be sympathetic to each other, share intelligence and contacts, and help each other up the ladder of success. On the lower rungs it often works this way. Why? The less you have, the less you feel you have to lose.

As you move from beginning writer to higher levels where you establish your name, gain professional credits, and earn money for your creative endeavors—and have the resources to help your fellow writers—something happens. And it's not good. Novelists, screenwriters, memoirists, poets, and journalists

"Half the game is ninety percent mental."
~ Yogi Berra

stop lending a hand to their fellow writers. From your now lofty position, helping the competition (or the perceived competition) is considered bad form. Do you really want to give your colleagues the power to leapfrog over you in the race for professional survival with your hard-won knowledge and connections?

Does that sound paranoid? Yes. Let's examine the pseudo-logic behind it.

1. If Writer A recommends Writer B, when Writer B's work turns out to be less-than-perfect (bear in mind that the publishing and movie industries are extremely subjective; what one exec deems brilliant another will call garbage), Writer A's taste is questioned and his reputation may take a hit. Is it worth the risk?

2. If Writer A introduces Writer B to their agent and the agent loves Writer B's work, Writer A looks good, but ultimately, Writer A receives less attention while Writer B's work is lauded.

I have been in both these situations. It made me angry. Happily, the anger fades. Let it go. I have helped many writers since then and the good experiences far outweigh the bad, but it doesn't feel like that at the moment your own agent is fawning over the Writer B you introduced while telling you that you need a comprehensive rewrite.

What many of us fail to recognize is that we have a relationship with our fellow writers. Not a commitment. We're not that

truths apply every-
everyone because the

a. Especially to you
nfortunately,   many

militant. Just a little give and take. Which is a big problem for the hungry scribe scrambling up the ladder. Most of them have nothing, which leaves them with no "give" and all "take." It also creates another demon that feeds the above problems: ingratitude.

In Los Angeles, a screenwriter acquaintance of mine survives as a reader (as many do). Her mantra: "If you help anyone, they just screw you over in the end." She complains at length about the number of times she has given out information and referrals and has not been repaid in kind, how others "owe her." She is, in my opinion, a lonely, bitter woman, refusing to help anyone but herself. Unfortunately for legions of writers, this selfish attitude is Hollywood gospel.

This hard-hearted view also exists in publishing circles, though it has not taken hold to the extent it has in the film business. In my soul, I don't believe that all writers are like my screenwriting acquaintance, but when I'm in L.A. it sure feels like it. I'm not trying to scare you or make you paranoid or selfish. I'm just warning you that negativity happens.

And negativity is deadly to writers. It distracts you from the true goal, writing. Which, in turn, will make you even more negative. It's the classic vicious circle. Unless you live in isolation, negativity is impossible to avoid. You must immunize yourself against it. How?

Adjust your actions, defeat ingratitude (learn to say thank you), and monitor your ego. We'll take these one at a time.

Adjust Your Actions

- It's not always about you. A bee goes to the flowers for the nectar. He doesn't know that he is serving the greater good by pollinating. The good of an action is often not seen by the person perpetuating it. Try anyway. Trust your instincts. Expect nothing in return. Be surprised if fruit shows up later.

- It's not action/reaction. Contacts aren't trading cards. "I'll show you mine if you show me yours" was cliché in kindergarten and it's a worse attitude now. Be generous. Go first. Hope for the best. Expect nothing.

- Learn to receive. It binds us together. If someone offers you a stick of gum or a lead on an agent, take it, thank them, and know that that is enough. You have shared something.

- Double dealing and sneaky tactics don't pay off in the long run. If you want an introduction to someone's agent, simply ask. They can always say no. Don't be offended. Never try to play them by offering information in hopes that they will return it in kind. Never pretend to have more star connections or experience than you have (you'll be found out and shunned).

- Always keep your mind and eyes open. Just as the bee doesn't know his effect on the world, often we don't either,

truths apply every-
everyone because the

a. Especially to you
nfortunately, many

but if you pay attention, sometimes you may catch a glimpse of the big picture.

Adjust Your Ego (Lies We Tell Ourselves)

- "I would have made it anyway." This sentence pops out of people you never thought it would. Many stunning books are still in desk drawers and will never see the light of day because no one is there to help. Be grateful. Give credit to those who help you.

- "I'll help when they prove themselves." Waiting for writers to get to your level before you help them is not helping them at all. Help now. It doesn't have to be dinner at your agent's house. Maybe it's just a sympathetic ear, a little encouragement, and a direction.

- "I can't help everyone that comes along." Fair enough. Just help some. Or one. Most people who say this sentence never help anyone.

- "No one helped me." If it's true, that's very sad. I haven't met a single, successful writer that hasn't had a lot of help. Some of it comes from other writers, some from agents, some from editors. Even if this sentence is true for you, break the chain and help others.

FOUR WAYS TO DEFEAT
INGRATITUDE

- When someone helps you, say "thank you." It's very simple, but many people forget.

- Send a thank-you card to the person who aided you. Hallmark is a huge corporation for a reason.

- Keep your mentor in the loop. Let them know that their contact was beneficial (even if just for the experience).

- Pass along the good deed. Even if you have limited contacts, share. If you help someone, let those who helped you know that you were inspired by them (it's the bee thing).

other hopefu
and waited f
my ten-minu
consult with
publishing
professional
longed to he
those magic
words, "Sen
the first fift
pages." It w
a validation
my self-wor
A reward fo
the long hou
I'd logged o
the chair, fa
ing my mon
tor, pecking
away at the
keys. More
than anythi
else in the
world, I was
determined
see my nam
in print on
cover of a
book. I was
going to be
world-
renowned
author. My
New York
Times best-
seller was ju
an agent aw

MANY EXECUTIVES ARE
INSECURE

It's nerve-racking sitting across from an executive who could make or break your writing dreams. You are face-to-face with someone who holds your future in his or her hands. You may have gotten a meeting through a friend of a friend at the executive's office. You may be at a conference. You may be waiting for a bus and the executive's Mercedes is in the shop. However it comes—and these chances do come—this is your chance to curry favor with the all-powerful Oz. So the executive listens to your story, then asks you …

"What's the inciting incident leading up to the climactic resolution of the truncated inversion point?"

What!? The incidental recitation of the resulting trunk and diversion point? Your mind reels, searching for meanings. Where did this come from? What does this exec know that you don't? Are you an idiot? Where's your answer? The executive stares, waiting.

Relax. They're insecure. Not only must they bring in commissions that justify their employment, the industry turnover rate is so high you'd think many literary agencies and management groups were Jiffy Lubes (change out execs every three months or three thousand manuscripts or screenplays). Editors are insecure, too. Many bounce from house to house, never really having a breakout acquisition that defines their career. If they don't cut it, sometimes they morph into agents. Agents turn managerial. Managers grow fangs, hairy upper arms, and howl at full moons until they transform into producers. Okay, I'm kidding. Most of them were producers all along, attaching themselves to their client's projects, hoping to split up the bounty once a project goes to film. All this career angst can make for some interesting meetings ... and questions.

So again, relax. These execs are showing off, trying to prove that they know as much about writing as you do. Which they generally don't. (Words are our lives. It's disheartening when they're turned against us!) Play along. Let them parade their ego around the room. Most execs are just letting you know that they attended the latest Bhagwan of Story Structure seminar in Los Angeles.

When all is said and done, all that matters is whether or not your story has potential for them. If you must answer the exec, stick with what you do know. Continue to pitch your story to the absolute best of your ability.

I've been through a lot of pitches. I've pitched at festivals. I've pitched at conferences. I've pitched in posh executive offices. I've pitched in cubicles, restaurants, bars, dog parks, at a race-track, in my home, and once, on an airplane. Sometimes I'm on my game. Sometimes I stink. Occasionally I'm ambushed by the mind-boggling exec question. How do I deal with it? I stick to the basics, and use my Executive Translation Dictionary (see page 96). Most jargon falls under these terms. And if you don't understand the question, simply ask, "Do you mean the turning point?"

Once you get beyond the catch-phrase phase of the conversation, you'll come to a very comforting realization. The executives are simply trying to communicate with us on what they perceive as our level. For everyone concerned and your career, it behooves you to make this as simple as possible.

TIPS FOR MAKING
A HUMAN CONNECTION

1. Leave your dog, Ego, at home.
If you don't understand something, ask.
Don't try to seem more important, educated,
or intelligent than you are. Don't try to "cover."
Be honest. People love to work with equals.

2. Ask questions.
It can build a bond between you and your audience. But never get too personal or ask too many
questions. Acceptable topics are sports ("Did you
see that game last night?"), food ("Have you
tried that new restaurant over on Fourth?"), or
business ("Did you hear that Disney is going to
restructure again?"). Note: Don't use that last
question if you are pitching a Disney exec.

3. Listen to the answers.
You may not believe that the twenty-year-old
executive across the desk from you has had
enough life experience to wax on about the
drawbacks of social security on the national
economy and his paycheck, but keep your mouth
shut. Nod along. Better yet, be fascinated.

room for ama
teurs or the
equipped.
Those alread
mining wag
from this
extremely co
petitive indu
try don't wa
to waste the
time on new
comers. And
you do show
promise, esta
lished autho
don't want
younger or
more talente
scribes vying
for jobs and
contacts on
their turf. T
door remain
closed to you
The process
finding some
one, other th
your mother
who will cha
pion your bo
takes on the
surreal feeli
of a high
school cafete
ria. The pop
lar kids han
out on one s

4. Make it seem like a conversation.

Conversations are made of give and take. Expect to give a lot more. Not words. Compassion, understanding, and empathetic rage if necessary. Listen to their extemporaneous speeches for as long as they run, then keep your responses brief, to the point, and witty (though not wittier than the executive). They may find you intriguing. It does happen. Just don't forget to pitch your story.

Remember, the goal is to connect. If you decide to work together, you're going to have a lot more conversations.

Sidebar text (left margin):

ling. All too well. I was once one of those writing conference writers. You know the type. Heart pounding and manuscript clutched to my chest, I lined up firing-squad-style with two dozen other hopefuls and waited for my ten-minute insult with a publishing professional. I longed to hear those magic words, "Send the first fifty pages." It was validation of my self-worth. A reward for the long hours I'd logged on the chair, facing my monitor, pecking away at the keys. More than anything else in the

THE EXECUTIVE TRANSLATION DICTIONARY
(OF TERMS WE CAN ALL AGREE ON)

Pitch. Your story in short form. Keep it as short as possible.

Logline. A synopsis of your story in one or two sentences.

Three-Act Structure. A story with a beginning, middle, and end.

Story Beats. Big events, twists, and character revelations in your story.

Turning Point. Something that happens and things change.

Protagonist. The good guy.

Antagonist. The bad guy.

room for am
teurs or the
equipped.
Those alreac
mining wag
from this
extremely cc
petitive indu
try don't wa
to waste the
time on new
comers. And
you do show
promise, est
lished autho
don't want
younger or
more talente
scribes vyin;
for jobs and
contacts on
their turf. T
door remain
closed to you
The process
finding som
one, other th
your mother
who will cha
pion your bo
takes on the
surreal feeli
of a high
school cafete
ria. The pop
lar kids han
out on one s

TRUTH #14

TO LIE IS WRONG;
TO EMBELLISH, DIVINE

A million years ago I worked as a résumé writer. Irv (name changed to protect the innocent), an unemployed pizza delivery dude, prevailed upon me to make him "look good" because his girlfriend was pregnant and he needed a better job in order to support his soon-to-be family. Sans high school diploma and any record of steady paychecks, I'll admit he was a challenge.

Glossing over the long stretches of unemployment with some creative travel opportunities, and spinning the pizza runs into "Nicola's Express Service—pickup and delivery of time-sensitive materials," Irv was on his way. Voilà! Fourteen days later he had a full-time position working for a courier service.

And something else happened that day too. A creative seed germinated between my ears. I was going to be a writer someday.

I'm not saying that what I did was entirely honest, but the intent behind the creative truth was good and it resulted in a win-win situation.

Whether you file lawsuits, flip burgers, punch numbers, or drive long haul, practice spinning your world to the creative side. Go to classes, write blogs, and volunteer with creative organizations while you work toward your goal.

PRESENT YOURSELF AS THE WRITER YOU WANT TO BE. BUT BE CAREFUL ...

An old Hollywood axiom says, "Bullshit is bullshit, but lying is wrong." This holds true in all areas of life and creative endeavors. You must know the difference between the steaming pile that actually has some basis and the outright untruth. Lying is wrong. The Bible says so. Enron executives may go to court for their falsehoods. There are penalties for it. Fortunately, the power of politics has prevailed and "spin," that favorite White House buzzword, will set you free. Therefore, to lie is wrong, but to embellish is divine.

If you are still in the beginning phases of getting an agent, getting your work read, and trying to make your first sale, the skill of lying-but-not-lying-creative-embellishment is imperative. You will use it in your résumé to make yourself look more professional. You'll use it in person to gain the positive attention

oom for amateurs or
d. Those already min-

stry don't want to
ime on newcomers.

of execs. And most of all, you will use it in your story pitch. Developing your passion, enthusiasm, and dynamic storytelling ability (even if you have to fake it) is the key to sparking the interest of the people who can set the wheels of your writing dreams in motion.

So You Think You've Got What It Takes

You've got a million-dollar story that has the potential to have you marching down red carpets of awards ceremonies. Great. You may have that story, but if you can't relay it succinctly to the agents, editors, and execs that hold your fate in their hands, your story could wind up collecting dust, not Academy Awards.

Fortunately, pitching your story is a lot like fishing. You need to hook your audience, play them a little, and then land them.

Hook

This is what stands out in your story. Think of it as the bait. It can be a character, a setting (time period or location), or an emotion. The following pitches are real. The names have been changed to protect me from the litigious.

Estelle spoke at length about the relationships within a family who had separated over the years until two siblings had no idea where the other was in the world. Toward the end of the pitch, she explained that the brothers, when they were finally united, were on opposite sides of a civil war. Interesting. Is that good enough? Probably not. The brothers are the heart of the story, but what is the hook? War. Conflict. Action.

> *The Lithuanian Civil War of 1716 was the bloodiest encounter in European history. Brother against brother. Two of these brothers were Rochelle and William Romaine.*

Let's look at a character hook.

> *Fred Canton is a handsome, thirty-year-old CPA at Barton Fink Schuster Accounting. Too bad he'll be falsely branded as a serial killer and dead in twenty-four hours.*

There's character, background, and consequences packed into two sentences. Or …

> *Mother Teresa had a great love for all people, especially one— her husband.*

Disturbing, but the exec should still be listening. The best hooks have a surprise. Brother battling brother. Accountant serial killers. Mother Teresa's secret marriage. Think of your story as tabloid news. What's your surprise? Find it.

A tale based on emotions is more difficult to make exciting since feelings are often quiet and internal. Introspection does not lend itself easily to action, but there's always a way.

A very proper British woman, Beatrice, pitched a lovely and intricate story of relationships and emotional reversals. Because it was far too lovely and intricate for the short pitch, she tried

'oom for amateurs or
d. Those already min-

stry don't want to
ime on newcomers.

something brazen. "My story is about love, jealousy, hate, pity, and how life can turn around and bite you on the ass."

This upright lady with her wonderful accent had started out quite normal and ended with "Bite you on the ahss." It was simply shocking. And charming. And risky. Did it work? Yes. The agent laughed, wanted to hear more, and requested the manuscript.

Phraseology

You're a writer. Words are gold. Construct Fort Knox. Use every alliteration, onomatopoeia, simile, and metaphor in your grammatical war chest to build a spectacle. Step right up and see the unbelievable, unrelenting eighth wonder of the world—your story. Make it exciting!

Don't say, "A boat hits a pier and catches fire." Use your imagination. Try something like, "The launch slams into the massive pilings. Deck boards splinter like toothpicks. Gas whooshes into flame as the dock, a sacrifice to the gods, blasts halfway to heaven in a ball of hellfire."

Avoid timid language: "Candace hesitates, starts to take a step toward the door, stops, rethinks the step she almost took, and slowly reaches for the handle." Yikes. Think, "Candace kicks a jackboot through the flimsy pine door." Pow. No loss of executive interest there.

Specifics

Name your characters. Maybe give them an occupation. An emotional angle. A detail here and there to make the sentence become a visual image. Focus on dynamic storytelling.

> *Bill Stewart, psychopathic dentist, has a birthmark the shape of Texas. To his chagrin and later cause of dementia, it's also the size of Texas.*

> *Babette and Francois, caustic teenage half-siblings, never knew that their paternal grandfather Pierre, one of the few things they had in common, was bricked up under the stairs of their Victorian home.*

Specifics build pictures to charm, shock, or amuse your target out of their passive existence. Think of what makes your story extraordinary.

oom for amateurs or
d. Those already min-

stry don't want to
ime on newcomers.

Heart pounding and manuscript clutched to my chest, I lined up firing-squad-style with two dozen other hopefuls and waited for my ten-minute consult with a publishing professional. I longed to hear those magic words, "Send the first fifty pages." It was validation of my self-worth. A reward for the long hours I'd logged on the chair, facing my monitor, pecking away at the keys. More than anything else in the world, I was determined to see my name in print on the cover of a book. I was going to be a

POP QUIZ
FOR PITCHING

Before you go in for the pitch, ask yourself these questions:

- Do you have a title?

- Do you know your genre?

- What's your Hook?

- Have you decorated your pitch with Phraseology and Specifics?

- Have you practiced saying your pitch at least a hundred times, and find yourself mumbling it in your sleep?

MOST-ASKED
PITCH QUESTIONS

How long is a pitch?

As short as possible. You need to give an accurate impression of the main characters, the genre, setting, story, conflicts, and maybe even a reversal or two. If you can sell your idea in one sentence, do it. If it takes a hundred, so be it. Every story has different demands. Your goal is to create a compelling impression of your story. You may encounter questions about the word count, page count, how long it took you to write your project, how long you've been marketing it, and to whom. If you know the answers, have them handy. But don't make them a part of your pitch.

Can I pitch more than one story?

There's a rule that states you should only pitch one project in any one sitting, but if your baby (your story) isn't wowing the crowd, switch babies. Use every shot you get.

What if I get nervous and screw up?

You will. Guaranteed. It's part of the process. A pitch is not life or death. It's just a pitch. Some go well.

experiences, including a stint as a wr ing conferen coordinator, met thousan of writers ju like me, all longing for their break. And I also found out th there are a series of cor truths, truth that writers must learn, accept and overcome if they hope to make it in p lishing. In fact, these truths apply everywhere and to every one because the industry a lot like the old high sch cafeteria. Especially to you new kid Unfortunate many writer who strive t make an

Some don't. Relish the good. Learn from your blunders.
Relax, forgive yourself, and improve. The executive
you flub to today will be replaced by someone you've
never heard of tomorrow. The more chances you take,
the more chances you get. So get comfortable. You
are in it for the long haul. The more you tell your
story, the easier and smoother it gets. Remember, it
only takes one "yes" to get things rolling.

What happens if they hate my story,
but love me?

A professional relationship is the next best thing
to a sale. Keep the door open. Follow up with a card.
Touch base every few months. Most writers have
more than one book or screenplay in them. You can
always pitch them your next story when it's ready.
Executives know this. Agent, editor, manager, lawyer
or producer … their goal is the same: to work with
people they like.

existed for decades. They are oblivious to the telltale signs that mark them as wannabes. Hence, the following Truths. I can't guarantee that insider know-

Through my experiences, ...ding a stint writing con... ...ce coordina-... I met thou-...ls of writers ...like me, all ...ng for their ... And I also ...nd out that ...are a series ...core truths, ...s that writ-...must learn, ...pt and over-...come if they ...e to make it ...blishing. In ...these truths ...apply every-...where and to ...one because ...ndustry is a ...like the old ...school cafe-...a. Especially ...u new kids.

WE ALL HAVE A LITTLE
OPERA DIVA
IN US

"The nice thing about egotists is that they don't talk about other people."
~Lucille S. Harper

It's not a crime to love yourself or your writing, but sometimes a story pitch to an executive can crash and burn in your first sentence. While you may indeed be the greatest writer who ever lived, no one is going to take you seriously if you come across as a self-important buffoon.

That said, your story is your baby. Rightfully so. It has taken a long time and a lot of effort to bring it to life. Yet to industry bean counters, your baby is nothing more than a *product*. So let's change your mindset to theirs and start calling your story a widget. That makes you a widget maker. You are a factory pumping out widgets. And the market for widgets is strong this year. The executives are going to be busy looking for all the widget makers they can find. Unfortunately, widget factories, like all other industries, have their crises too. The culprit is usually staff and management problems. That means you. There are certain personalities, big ones, strange ones, and downright scary ones, that make executives want to run screaming away no matter how great the story may be.

At any social gathering there's guaranteed to be one of these people in every room. He or she is the loudmouth at a writers conference, in a wine bar, or anywhere people assemble. Although their motives may be good, these people carry on conversations decibels above everyone else. They never tire of their own voice, and a melodic lyric of "Me-me-me-me" would qualify them for a starring role in an opera.

It's called ego. Ego is a defense mechanism that Homo sapiens have carried inside since prehistoric times. Scientists suspect that it was used to protect man from sarcastic mastodons. We also have an appendix from that era. Neither is of much use when you're pitching your project.

Be warned of the following personalities that can lurk in the shadows of our psyches, then jump out and ruin any shot we may have had at selling our story.

The Opera Diva

This poisonous personality isn't fatal, but you do need to put a cork in it. Too much information on any subject, especially your favorite one—you—will turn everyone off. Here's a test: If a

el like you are on the
g in at your success-

you ever attended a
ence, book signing or

horn blasted every time you say "I," would your conversation drown in the racket?

Ancient Annie

Skip the history lesson and stay current. There is no need to relive the game-saving tackle, the marriage proposal from the Italian count who was only after your money, or your first-place win in the World Poetry Competition of 1976. Writing a memoir? If the incident is pertinent, use it. Then move on to who you are now. Quickly.

The Overachiever

While you may think of yourself and your accomplishments as riveting, be assured the rest of the world does not. Endeavor to keep conversations flowing. How? Focus on subjects that relate to the greater good of mankind, not how your work has changed the lives of thousands. Don't recite your busy schedule of events. Don't give us endless details of your most recent successes. Even if you've been nominated for sainthood, let your actions (and writing) speak louder than spoken words.

Timid Tess

Shyness, while sometimes cute, will not get your story or your pertinent personal information across to those who need it. If you must take an acting class to come out of your shell, do it. Communication is mandatory.

The Rambler

Conversations loop. You connect from one topic to another and finally wrap up where you started. Well, stop it. Know what you are going to say. Say it. Then shut up. Don't get distracted. Don't get sidetracked. Don't backtrack because you forgot to mention something you were supposed to say at the beginning of your story. Keep moving. Forward.

The Gambler

You think they'll never ask to see your work so you pitch, pitch, pitch away. Of course, there is no work to show. Self-deception is a wonderful game to play—until they actually ask to see something. Whoops. You meant to write that screenplay you are pitching, but never quite got around to putting it down on paper. Fortunately, there is a cure for you: Lay off the pitching circuit, stop pretending you are a writer, and knuckle down to the page.

The Lord's Anointed One

God personally told you to write this book. And now you want to share this revelation with the world. Keep it to yourself. You are a widget factory. The customer doesn't care how the widgets are made or who told you to make them, they just want their damn widgets. Besides, the God-made-me-write-it angle is so common these days it has become a cliché.

el like you are on the
g in at your success-

you ever attended a
ence, book signing or

The Cross-Examiner

Your pitch isn't really a pitch, but more of an interrogation. You start off conversations with, "How many books did you really sell last year?" or, "Weren't you surprised when your hundred-million-dollar-movie only made a hundred thousand at the box office?" And that's before you get personal, trying to suck out the intimate details of their lives. While some are offended by you and others tell you to MYOB, most will sit quietly and calmly, knowing that your widgets will never be invited through their door again.

Supplicant Sam

You will do anything to ingratiate yourself. Need a cup of coffee? No problem. A ride to the airport? Sure thing. A blood transfusion? Okeydokey. You are nothing. Agents, editors, and producers are your gods. You may get information from your gods, but you will never get their respect. Instead, try treating everyone, including yourself, as an equal.

The Damsel of Desperation

Congratulations, you have replaced your low self-esteem with a four-hundred-page manuscript. And it must find love at any cost. Since your ego is still attached by an umbilical cord to your work, you are easily hurt. Maybe that self-esteem transplant didn't work. Get therapy. Get some distance. Your work is NOT you.

If you need love, try a dating service. If you want an honest evaluation of your manuscript, suck it up and face down your fears.

The Topper

Whatever anybody else in the room has done, you've done it better, longer, smarter, and faster. If someone tells you they had a baby, you immediately exclaim, "I had twins." Similarly, if the person you're pitching has sold a book or won a prize, congratulate them and skip your own awards list. Life is not a competition.

The Writer-Christ

Writers suffer. Especially you. You get little recognition and even less respect. Everyone is out to take advantage of you. And that's okay. It's your burden to bear. There may well be a cross out there with your name on it, but guess what? Nobody cares. If you get crucified on your way to success, and you most probably will, go whine to your loved ones … not the agents, not editors, not producers. They already have their crucifixion appointment books filled.

el like you are on the
g in at your success-

you ever attended a
ence, book signing or

ASS KISSERS ARE LOVED

> "The more people you know, the better your chances are for being heard."
> ~Ashley Kraas

Success is 80 percent who you know. And the more people who know and like you can quickly translate into opportunities. Yet it doesn't help if they can't remember your name.

Fortunately, ass kissing in the publishing and movie industries is a time-honored tradition. It's a stratospherically elevated form of flattery. Subtle flattery. It is so deeply entrenched in its denizens that many outsiders think the business is a really great "happy-happy-nice-land" place to do business. It's not. So what does all this have to do with getting you to the royal ball? Slow down, Cinderella, your pumpkin coach has been temporarily delayed until you learn to kiss ass ... then you can dance the night away.

But first, be aware that ...

BROWNNOSERS ARE HATED.

What? They're the same!

Not quite. It's a matter of degree. And pressure. There is no question in your mind when you meet a brownnoser. You feel it. It's cloying. Intrusive. Everyone despises the "yes man." After a professional ass kissing, the Kissee usually has a feeling of well-being, confidence, and, not too surprisingly, has developed an affinity for your company. The Kissee shouldn't be aware that his ass has been kissed. It's stealth.

In order to become part of these worlds you're going to have to get out there and network, make connections, and shrewdly ass kiss your way to the next level. (Sorry, talent alone rarely cuts it.) How?

Rules to Schmooze By

1. Never begin a conversation by pitching your story. It makes you look like an amateur and it drives people away.

2. "Hi, my name is _____. What do you do?" This may be an effective opening for gold diggers on the make for sugar daddies, but it does not belong at parties, premieres, conferences, or anywhere else. It's awkward. It's insincere. Find something, anything, that you have in common. "Was that chicken or shoe leather we had for lunch?" "That's a great suit. I love wool." "How about those Cardinals?"

eling. All too well. I
of those writing con-

ng and manuscript
y chest, I lined up

(You can be talking sports, birds, or the Catholic church with this one.)

3. If possible, stay on your feet during cocktails. This is called networking. Should you get cornered by someone you'd rather not speak with, it can be difficult to make a hasty exit while seated.

4. It's okay to praise a person's accomplishments if you actually know what you're talking about. Generic compliments like, "I love your work," fall on deaf ears. They've heard it a zillion times before. Don't tell a famous author you loved his book when you haven't read past page five. Don't tell someone you've seen their movie when you haven't.

5. Let them know you respect their choices or work, then move on to common denominators that have nothing to do with the industry. Sports, pets, fashion, food, travel, anything other than the industry. The goal is to get to know others on a human level, so …

6. Always ask questions. Find out what they are passionate about.

7. Listen to their answers. Make mental notes. You'll need them for the next time you meet.

8. Don't bludgeon your audience with your fascinating personal history. Let them draw you out. Don't tell them

absolutely everything about yourself and what you know. Reveal information in a timely manner.

9. Speak appropriately. Don't act like you are an insider if you aren't. You will get caught.

10. Never do the stare-through. Not happy with the person you're ass kissing? For heaven's sake move on. Polite conversation does not include staring through the person you are speaking with, keeping an eye on the door to see if some bigger game wanders in.

11. If you are on the receiving end of the "stare-through," either call them on it or politely excuse yourself from the conversation and move on to people who do want to talk to you. Agents and other high-powered execs are often repeat offenders of the stare-through.

12. Keep a friendly, though professional distance. If someone has spilled a drink on himself, has a sprig of parsley hanging from one bicuspid, mussed-up hair, smudged lipstick, an untucked shirt, or an open fly, it is not your job to make improvements in another's grooming. It is socially presumptuous. You can discreetly mention the parsley and the open zipper if you are alone with that person, but do not point at or touch body parts. It's crossing the line.

13. On a similar subject, resist the urge to "mother." One kind-hearted conference coordinator I know lurches through

eling. All too well. I
of those writing con-

ig and manuscript
y chest, I lined up

hotel hallways with papers flying out of his briefcase, wrinkled shirt untucked, mad-professor hair, and eyeglasses askew. Everyone on the staff loves and accepts him for who he is (and we also know he has been up all night taking care of last-minute details). He's a wreck. Yet the man is simply a magnet for the maternally inclined. Middle-aged to elderly women, all strangers, come at him from every angle, bent on executing a cosmetic improvement or two.

14. If you are asked about what you write, keep it brief. Memorize a killer logline or two that will leave them wanting more. If an agent, editor, or manager asks for more, offer to meet with them at a later time or send the material to them.

15. Do not name drop excessively. It's a sure sign of a brownnoser.

16. If the agent or executive who you're talking with is only looking for thrillers and you write romantic comedy, don't try to convince him he is looking for romantic comedy. If possible, don't pitch at all.

17. If you are speaking with the thriller-seeking executive above and a member of your critique group wrote one, you would be remiss not to mention that information. This is how you build relationships with people. Help your fellow writers.

18. Know when it's time to leave. When is that? Before it's time to leave. Remember, later you will follow up with a call, e-mail or letter.

AUTOGRAPH PROTOCOL

Writers flock to published authors. They line up to get books autographed and have their photos taken. But some fans don't stop there. When you get the opportunity to meet with an author at a book signing, be courteous and observe these rules:

1. Do not cut in line in front of everyone else just because you have an appointment somewhere else in ten minutes. Don't cut in line for any reason.

2. If there's a line of people waiting behind you, keep your conversation brief.

3. Do not ask the author out for drinks or to your family reunion. They have their own lives. Signing a book does not obligate them to be part of your life.

4. Exception to the above: Sometimes you can ask the author out on a "meet-for-coffee" date. My single author friends insisted that I add this tidbit. But since this area goes beyond the usual

feeling intim dated by the seemingly insurmount- able wall of people who a already in th game? It doe n't seem fair. It's not. The publishing world is toug to crack. Wh you are in th early stages getting peopl to notice you talent, earnin a living through you creative endeavors is like trying to climb Everes with a roll of tooth floss ar thumb tacks for spikes. There is no room for ama teurs or the equipped. Those alread mining wage from this extremely co petitive indu

autograph protocols, I suppose the usual rules of
flirtation would apply.

5. You're not obligated to buy a book. Sure, it's a
nice show of support, but just having the ability
to fog a mirror and show up at the book signing
is enough to warm most authors' hearts.
Thousands of book-signing events go virtually
unattended, and trust me, there is nothing sadder
than an author sitting alone at a table, stack of
books at the ready.

6. NEVER NEVER NEVER ask an author to read
your book/chapter/poem or any other type of writing. Never insist that they must write a glowing
review for your book/chapter/poem/whatever. They
won't. And while you can ask who their agent is,
don't expect them to fork over their agent's home
address and telephone number.

their time on newcomers. And if you do show promise, established authors don't want younger or more
talented scribes vying for jobs and contacts on their

New York
es bestseller
was just an
gent away.
, somebody
d recognize
my talent,
lling errors
ll. This was
ite the little
ntasy I had
ng between
ears. I did
published…
ntually. But
etting from
eamland to
y, and actu-
seeing my
ne in print,
s an adven-
in discover-
he customs
oreign land
blishing). I
ned to keep
networking
lar on at all

TRUTH #17

MUTTON DRESSED UP AS LAMB IS STILL MUTTON

Dye jobs, tummy tucks, hair plugs, Wonderbras, gym memberships, Beverly Hills Diet juice and gut-sucking girdles. If it makes us look and feel younger, thinner, or better about ourselves, we want it. Especially if we are "writers over a certain age" marketing our work.

As I write this missive, the maximum acceptable age for Hollywood movers and shakers is 24.71 years of age and shrinking fast. *Thirteen*, the Oscar-nominated movie, was cowritten by teenager Nikki Reed. At age sixteen, Nick McDonell received a six-figure advance for his first novel, *Twelve*. These scribes just keep getting younger and younger.

Like a digital countdown clock, that maximum acceptable age shrinks every second. By the time this book is published there is a good chance that some embryonic egg, sprung from the loins of a major director and nepotistically ushered into the ranks of power will be nominated for an Emmy.

So before you launch another round of "Frank McCourt (*Angela's Ashes*) did it," you should take heed. McCourt is rare. If you are over thirty, you have every reason to worry. By the time you've learned the craft of writing, you may have passed the Southern California salable talent expiration date. And by "you," I unfortunately mean "we." Is it any wonder that we are driven to the manmade fountains of youth? Our work, our babies that we have spent months, years, and decades creating, are in danger because Mommy or Daddy developed laugh lines and gray hair.

Fortunately, we're tenacious. We're skilled. And we're devious. Nobody messes with our babies. Not even Father Time. We still have a few tricks left up the sleeves that cover our wobbly upper arms. And like touching up our roots every month, staying current in the creative market is a matter of maintenance.

While I can't give you an exact list of what to wear, there are guidelines. Since good, clean writing is a writer's goal, your clothing and personal style should reflect that. You are selling your writing. You are selling you. By showing the pros that you have respect for yourself, you are showing them that you respect their time. The basic rule here is simple does it. When you leave, you want them to talk about what you wrote, not what you wore. Here are a few tips on how to market yourself at any age.

experiences, includ-
a writing conference

e me, all longing for
nd I also found out

Stay Current in Any Decade

Keep your writing voice fresh by staying culturally current. In the August 2003 issue of *Writer's Digest*, best-selling author Janet Evanovich admits she must bridge the decades-wide age gap between herself and her protagonist, twenty-something Stephanie Plum. "There's a danger in writing a character who's a generation removed from you," she says. Turning to her daughter Alex, Evanovich keeps Steph's slang and speech current and her wardrobe up to date—tight jeans, leather boots, and all.

Writing about history? Study recently released books and movies based on past events. While it may be historically correct to use the slang of that era in your dialogue, allow your modern-day audience to make a connection in this century. As language evolves, some terms are left in the dust. "23 skidoo" and "cat's pajamas" may not fly in today's market, but then again, "peace out, brother" may be out of vogue in another decade too. Be a classic. Clothing styles may change, but the basic forms of our language remain the same. Write in clear, simple language that will be understood a hundred years from now.

Align Yourself With the Young and Successful

Never compare yourself or your work to Barbara Cartland. The masterfully talented grand dame of the romance novel was a legend in her time. The key word here is "was." In fact, never compare yourself to any dead author. It's bad form. If you're "current" you should be able to find a successful screenwriter or author, one with recent credits, to whom you can liken your work.

And never compare yourself to reclusive, difficult, non-name-brand or mildly successful authors.

Get The Right Agent

Feeling a little damp under the arms when you discover that the person who requested your work is a nineteen-year-old college intern? Imagine how awful it must be for the once-famous to take meetings with a new regime of power kids all under thirty years old. No wonder the shrewd flee Hollywood at a certain age and let their agents battle out twilight careers for them. It's a dog-eat-dog world out there. Be prepared to hide in the shadows and let your representation get bitten in the ass for you.

So who's your champion now? There are two ways to go. You can hook up with the new talent. Yep, sign with that stage-diving, Ecstasy-popping wunderkind who can usher your work into the studio offices of stage-diving, Ecstasy-popping producers. Or …

Focus on professionals with years of experience and sales to reputable players who have been established for decades. The pubescent producers of teen flicks are not looking for a WWII epic (at least not until the next battle saga breaks one-hundred million at the box office on opening weekend). If you stick to the execs with life experience and reputable sales to their credit, you can't

experiences, includ-
a writing conference

e me, all longing for
nd I also found out

go wrong. They are the ones who will appreciate your unique experiences and talent.

I prefer the second choice.

Repackage Your Sizzle

Go ahead, join Weight Watchers, hop on a treadmill, or lift weights. Whatever you have to do to feel more confident is bound to increase your chances of success. It's not because it makes you a better writer, but because it helps you embrace the possibilities life holds. Face it, how we feel about ourselves shows in our work. Sometimes we need to resort to a little external help.

To keep myself in check, I limit my self-improvements to the extra money in my budget that has come from writing. That almost covers a monthly bottle of Miss Clairol. Instead of a gym membership, I try to walk an hour a day. That hour sacrifice keeps me from panting and puffing into meetings, plus it's a great diversion when I'm not quite ready to face the page.

If you're considering more extreme measures, remember we're writers, not movie stars. I'm not saying facelifts, tummy tucks, and hair transplants are out of the question, but these self-improvements won't sell your project, so make sure that your prose remains larger than your new look.

Dress Appropriately

There is nothing as bad as trying too hard. A friend of mine refers to the epidemic of women who dress decades younger than their age, or in another era, as "mutton dressed up as lamb." Men are at risk too. A fringed and studded leather ensemble might have made you a chick magnet in the 1960s, but it won't help you sell your project in this decade.

Don't overdress or underdress. Carrie Bradshaw (*Sex and the City*) wanna-bes of any age need to be careful too. Sarah Jessica Parker carried off the look for years, but only with the help of a wardrobe staff and top designers.

experiences, includ-
a writing conference

e me, all longing for
nd I also found out

TIPS FOR DRESSING:
WOMEN

- Nix outlandish jewelry.

- Bizarre hats should stay in the closet.

- Avoid floral arrangements on any part of the body.

- Skip the cleavage-revealing outfits.

- Midriff-baring clothing is already passé. And if you're past your teen years or weigh more than a coat rack, they don't want to see your navel.

- Crotch-baring skirts (just forget you ever saw *Basic Instinct*) will not do anything for your career. They really don't want to see it.

- The devil wears Prada ... and you can too. Just make sure your designer wear is simple and tasteful. This is not the time to break out the rainbow-feathered couture number you bought in Paris.

eling. All too well. I was once one of those writing conference writers. You know the type. Heart pounding and manuscript clutched to my chest, I lined up firing-squad-style with two dozen other hopefuls and waited for my ten-minute consult with a publishing professional. I longed to hear those magic words, "Send the first fifty pages." It was validation of my self-worth. A reward for the long hours I'd logged on the chair, facing my monitor, pecking away at the keys. More than anything else in the

- Again, skip obvious jewelry.
- Baseball hats are acceptable ... outside.
- Power suits are for power players. Tom Wolfe wears a white suit with style, but most authors and screenwriters lean toward casual wear for meetings. The rule of thumb on suits is that if you only wear them for weddings and funerals, you should not don one for a creative meeting.
- Too casual won't work either. Tie-dye T-shirts, frayed cutoffs, and ratty Birkenstocks should be left at home. In some regions, like Hawaii, T-shirts, shorts, and sandals are perfectly acceptable. Think clean and tidy.
- If you're inside, take off the sunglasses.

petitive indu try don't war to waste thei time on new-comers. And you do show promise, esta lished author don't want younger or more talente scribes vying for jobs and contacts on their turf. T door remains closed to you The process finding some one, other th your mother who will cha pion your bo takes on the surreal feeli of a high school cafete ria. The pop lar kids han out on one s of the room and the dweebs, nerd geeks, a.k.a. the writers.. you... cower the other.

TIPS FOR DRESSING: COUPLES, WRITING PARTNERS, AND REALLY CREATIVE TYPES

- Silly costumes are off-limits. Shakespeare's works still sell well in this day and age, but dressing as a poofy-pantalooned bard won't win you any points. In fact, you might scare people off.
- Religious garb, kilts, saris, shillelaghs, military clothing, lederhosen, Kevlar vests, and tiaras: If it's ceremonial or decorative, leave it in the closet. If your line of work requires you to wear the item on a daily basis, use your common sense. If it's something you wear on a daily basis because of your ethnic heritage or beliefs, go for it.
- "Bobbsey Twins" routines are corny. Do not dress alike.
- Park all laptops. Portable computers belong in your briefcase. Agents spend enough time looking at computer screens. They don't want to see your files, film trailers, naked JPGs, or any other visual displays.

eling. All too well. I was once one of those writing conference writers. You now the type. Heart pound- g and manu- cript clutched o my chest, I ed up firing-squad-style th two dozen ther hopefuls nd waited for y ten-minute onsult with a publishing rofessional. I nged to hear those magic words, "Send the first fifty ages." It was validation of y self-worth. A reward for e long hours I'd logged on he chair, fac- ng my moni-tor, pecking away at the keys. More an anything else in the

ing away at
keys. More
n anything
1 the world,
determined
ee my name
print on the
of a book. I
vas going to
be a world-
renowned
or. My New
Times best-
ler was just
agent away.
y, somebody
d recognize
my talent,
lling errors
ll. This was
ite the little
ntasy I had
ing between
y ears. I did
published…
ntually. But
etting from
reamland to

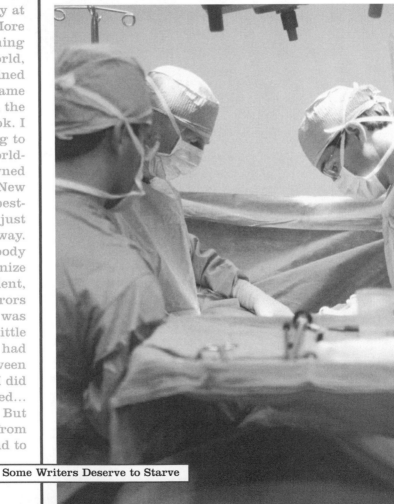

HIRING A PRO DOESN'T
GUARANTEE SUCCESS

"Some editors are failed writers, but so are most writers."
~T.S. Eliot

Where there is art, there is commerce. Some reputable. Some not. Manuscript editing and creative consulting is big business, raking in millions of dollars annually. From national corporations with editing services to authors and private individuals with a handful of credits to their name, thousands of writers out there, for a fee, are availing themselves to other writers. And the majority of them are honest people with your best interests at heart.

Unfortunately, everyone has heard tales of writers being unwittingly taken advantage of by the unscrupulous. Writers have paid thousands of dollars in the hope that the skilled eye of a freelance editor will somehow fix their project—only to wind up with a few dozen photocopied pages of advice and an empty bank account. Literary agents charge their clients hundreds of dollars to edit manuscripts that will never be read by publishing houses. Screenwriters bitten by the Oscar bug, cough up big money to have a pro read their work, yet receive little more than a few scribbled notes in the margins. This isn't help. But this is not to say that hiring outside help isn't a good idea.

"It's never a bad idea to have a professional reading before the work is sent out to the universe, just to test the waters," says Nancy Hardin, producer of the Oscar-winning movie *Frida*. "It's essential for a writer to get, at the very least, one second opinion on what he or she has written because there is no way the writer won't be so close to the work that some pretty major problems, or even just plain mistakes, might not be overlooked."

What's a writer to do? How do you discern the difference between a con artist and an editor who will aid you in becoming the best writer you can be?

Ed Griffin, a creative writing instructor in a maximum-security prison and author of two self-published books, had been working on his first novel for seventeen years. Enough was enough. For almost two decades he'd tried to make sense of his protagonist's emotional arc while fleshing out the minor characters. Pragmatic by nature, Ed was stumped when it came to making the dialogue of his female lead believable. Ed knew he needed help.

The freelance editor who took on his project was a published author and well-known speaker: Her client roster boasted over a dozen success stories that led to book deals. But her several-dollars-per-page fee was steeper than Ed expected. The final cost was several hundred dollars—all for a twenty-page-long critique.

Was it worth it? Ed thought so. He spent another six months at the keys making changes. Though *Prisoners of the Williwaw* did not sell to a publisher, it was optioned by HBO films.

Seventeen years is a long stretch for any project. Longer than many marriages. So why couldn't Ed teach himself everything he needed to know about writing in that amount of time? Because everyone evolves at his or her own pace. Many of us work day jobs and raise families. We simply don't have the time to be as prolific as we'd like to be, to learn everything we need to know about the craft of writing. And sometimes knowing when to buy professional guidance can mean the difference between a sale, like Ed's, and another manuscript sitting in a drawer collecting dust. Sometimes writing takes more than commitment. It takes a pro.

But before you crack open your checkbook, let's see if you are ready for the red pen of a professional freelance editor. Ask yourself the following questions:

1. Have you finished your manuscript or screenplay?

If you don't know where your story is going, or you know but you haven't gotten around to writing it down yet, the pro cannot help you. Do not consider a book doctor or editing service before you finish your manuscript or screenplay. If you have a completed work, proceed.

2. What level of rejections are you receiving?

Do you receive photocopied form letters rejecting your work? Or do they contain comments about the piece you wrote, encouraging words, or invitations to resend the work after another polish?

In the beginning, our words usually get little notice. If we're lucky, the standard form letter comes back in our SASE. As we progress, the rejection letters become more personalized. Agents have radar for good writing. They know how much effort it takes to craft a well-written piece. If they respect the effort you've put into your work, they will respond graciously, often offering comments.

If you are still in the form-letter phase, go back to the keyboard and polish your prose. You are not ready for a professional edit. On the other hand, if your rejections include …

- invitations to call/e-mail the agent to discuss your other projects
- a request for you to resend your work after you make changes
- story-specific comments on how you can improve

… then you've caught their attention. Congratulations.

If you still aren't sure if you've made it out of the form-letter phase, take a chance and don't send a self-addressed stamped envelope with your query or requested work. If an agent likes what you've got, they will call or e-mail you. No reply should be considered a pass.

MANY AGENTS BOAST THAT THEY CAN TELL WHETHER OR NOT A WRITER CAN WRITE BY THE QUERY LETTER ALONE.

3. Have you written to the absolute best of your ability?

Have you drummed out every single run-on sentence and extraneous adverb? Have you edited so many drafts that you are blind to pronoun omissions? Do you feel that you cannot expand or better your work beyond what you have in front of you?

If you answered "yes" to all of the above questions, good. Respected editors and consultants do not have time to dillydally with the work of amateurs. True professionals aren't paid to lecture you on how to use language. They are like Olympic trainers. Their job is to take your near-professional-quality writing and aid you in muscling it out to a gold-medal-contender status that will awe the judges.

4. Do you sometimes wish that elves would steal into your home in the middle of the night and finish editing your book or script for you?

(Hey, don't laugh. This is my recurring fantasy!) Good news. If you've arrived at this point, you are only suffering from a mild case of burnout. Your manuscript is complete, but you, being the perfectionist that you are, insist that only your best work can go out the door. The work ahead is intimidating, but you push on anyway, getting it done a paragraph or line at a time. Professional help from a writing consultant will most likely make your work even better. In the meantime, go ahead and indulge in your favorite editing-elf fantasies.

The Professionals

Before purchasing editing services, understand that editors and consultants play two basic roles when it comes to guiding writers toward professional careers. Which pro does your work need?

The Line Editor

Line editors provide services for manuscripts in need of a thorough cleaning. A line editor is a housekeeper for your novel or nonfiction book. Their job is to sweep through the chapters, straighten out grammar, vacuum excess language from the pages, pick up those superfluous commas, suggest stronger verbs, and make your prose spic and span.

g world is tough to
you are in the early

earning a living
creative endeavors is

The Book Doctor

The book doctor, sometimes known as a script consultant, is more of a surgeon than a general MD. Though he can immunize manuscripts against common maladies such as weak protagonists and poor circulation between chapters and acts, his best skills are with the scalpel. Cutting deep, the doctor probes voice, style, plotting, and emotional arcs. These operations cannot save terminal prose. Patient and project must be in good health before this invasive procedure is performed.

Contacting a Pro

Conferences, writing-related Web sites, the Association of Author Representatives, and nonprofit writing organizations all have recommendations for book editing services. Another useful resource is the *National Directory of Editors and Writers For Hire*, published by M. Evans & Co. As always, ask potential editors for credentials and verify them before you make any major decisions.

When you do find someone you'd like to hire, expect to send a partial manuscript to them for a checkup (usually for a flat fee, a fraction of what a full edit/critique would cost). Like any physician (or housekeeper for that matter), the good ones are often backed up for months. There are waiting lists, and top-rated pros don't have time to perform surgery on patients who aren't ready for the operating room. You must be a patient

patient. Once your pages pass the initial examination, the doctor may screen you further to make sure you are really ready. These talented people do not waste their time on bad writing or temperamental personalities.

g world is tough to
you are in the early

earning a living
creative endeavors is

WHAT YOU CANNOT EXPECT FROM A PRO

Professional help is not a shortcut.

Do not expect your manuscript or screenplay to come back to you as a perfect specimen. Be prepared to work hard, probably for several months, integrating your consultant's comments and suggestions into your work.

Professional help is not praise.

Don't expect the editor to proclaim your work a pleasure to read and insist on refunding your money because your talent is clearly exceptional. If you want love and acceptance, get a dog. These services are for writers who sincerely desire an honest, professional opinion and can accept criticism and comments with an open mind.

Professional help is not access to an editor's Rolodex.

Although some editors will scout manuscripts for agents and producers, the odds of them passing your work to higher-ups are slim. It does happen. Sometimes. Just don't count on it. Paying a pro for a critique doesn't mean that they are obligated to stamp their personal "recommend" on your project.

TERMS USED BY THE PROS

While there are two basic types of professional editors, various services may be offered. Here's a rundown on some of the terms you'll hear.

Proofread. A proofread zeroes in on spelling mistakes, typos, and misaligned verb tenses. It's a basic but intensive look at each and every word on the page.

Line Edit. A step beyond the proofread, a line edit will focus on flow and logic. This process will aid the writer in taking the language of the project to a higher level.

Content Edit. This is sometimes called a developmental edit. It's a broad view of the project. Mood, tone, pace, metaphor, theme, subtlety, and character motivation are examined, as are the underpinnings of structure and conflict.

just an agen
away. Surely
somebody
would recog
nize my tale
spelling err
and all. This
was quite th
little fantasy
had playing
between my
ears. I did g
published…
ntually. But
getting from
dreamland t
reality, and
actually see
my name in
print, was a
adventure ir
discovering
customs of a
foreign land
(publishing)
learned to k
my network
ing radar or
all times (yo
never know
who you wil
meet) and,
most of all,
face the fact
that the mo
tain I was tr
ing to climb

experiences,
including a
nt as a writ-
g conference
oordinator, I
et thousands
' writers just
like me, all
longing for
their break.
And I also
und out that
there are a
series of core
ruths, truths
that writers
must learn,
accept and
overcome if
they hope to
ke it in pub-
lishing. In
fact, these
truths apply
everywhere
and to every-
one because
e industry is
a lot like the
old high
school cafete-
a. Especially
to you new
kids.
nfortunately,
nany writers
who strive to

Coverage. Used for scripts, coverage is the term used to describe the one- or two-page synopsis written by a professional reader who is hired by a studio or production company. "Coverage" is also sold to writers by magazines, Web sites, and individuals claiming to have connections to studios and production companies. Some are legit. Some aren't.

Analysis. Again, this is a term used in screenwriting circles. Analysis is in-depth. Structure, dialogue, characters, and emotional arcs are put under the microscope. Depending on the service, this type of critique can be pages of detailed comments or scribbled notes in the margins of your script.

Mentoring. Not all writers or manuscripts are ready for review. That's where mentoring comes in. Some editors offer personal coaching services. They will help you develop a game plan, assist in plotting out scenes, and keep you and your project on track.

you do show
promise, estab-
lished authors
don't want
larger or more
talented scribes
vying for jobs
& contacts on
their turf. The
door remains
closed to you.
The process of
finding someone,
other than your
mother, who will
champion your
book takes on
a surreal feel-
ing of a high
school cafeteria.
The popular kids
hang out on one
side of the room
and the dweebs,
nerds, geeks,
a.k.a. the writ-
ers... you...
cower on the

SOME AGENTS
ARE DISHONEST
FROM THE GET-GO

"Now, now, my good man, this is no time for making enemies."
~ Voltaire

Wherever would-be scribes gather, the collective I need an agent" bleat is deafening. Even the youngest scribes among us have their radar set for literary representation. At a recent brunch I attended, I sat next to a seventeen-year-old playwright, author of two high school–produced one-act plays, who insisted that she "had to" secure an agent before she entered college. It was on her "to do" list— right after a new cell phone and before getting her teeth capped.

So many writers today rush into the search for representation. Why not? It's thrilling to have a professional take an interest in your work and consider it a marketable product. Yet the majority of writers are disappointed when they don't find an agent right away. They get discouraged. And worse yet, they make foolish choices and fall victim to agents who are dishonest from the get-go.

I refer to this unscrupulous part of the industry as the pirate side. According to Victoria Strauss and A.C. Crispin, founders of the Science Fiction Writers of America's Committee on Writing Scams, writers should be cautious of "services sending a synopsis and other information about your work to publishing houses via printed or electronic catalogue. We know of no publishers that look at these materials." In my experience, this looks cheap and it demonstrates that the agent isn't confident that the work will sell. These agencies often charge fees. "Even if you get a fee charger to send your manuscript in, we won't take it seriously. Most of the time, we don't even open these submissions," notes Laura Anne Gilman of Roc, an imprint of Penguin, in the August 2003 issue of *Writer's Digest.* Finally, these buccaneers "shotgun" projects out to publishers and producers. Lacking established industry relationships (relationships formed by industry experience and sales), they blindly submit the work to anyone and everyone … and wait months for a response, if they receive one at all.

AGENTS WITH PRODUCTIVE, ESTABLISHED CONNECTIONS RECEIVE QUICK TURNAROUND FROM EDITORS: ANYWHERE FROM AN OVERNIGHT READ TO A FEW WEEKS.

nd out that there are
e truths, truths that

ope to make it in pub-
t, these truths apply

For many writers, even professional ones who are already making money in the industry, signing with an agent can sometimes take years. A friend of mine is an author and playwright. His plays were performed regularly at the Actors Studio in New York City. He was hired to write a screenplay for a French company. They flew him to France, covered his living expenses, and gave him a generous income for months. Did he have an agent? Nope, though he did get one eventually. With the help of his agent, he sold his first novel, which was later turned into a movie. Within a few years, he was regularly writing television and movie scripts for Hollywood.

I've known my agent since 2000. I met her at a writing conference where I was volunteering at the consult check-in desk. When one of her appointments failed to show, she wandered into the hallway, bored, and asked me what I wrote. Fortunately, I had a killer pitch memorized and she asked for one hundred pages right away. Pretty cool, huh? You'd think the rest would be history. It wasn't. I kept in contact with her for three years before she officially offered me representation. During those three years I had a book published, I wrote a column, and I was getting paid to write (granted, I wasn't making a fortune, but it was still an income).

So where does that leave honest writers seeking honest representation? The answer is not one you're going to want to hear. Finding an agent who will represent your project is a task that equals, if not exceeds, the challenges of learning the craft or writing and penning a book. While I can't guarantee that each and every one of us has a well-written, lively yet thought-provoking manuscript that oozes mass appeal, I can give you an edge when it comes time to embark on the agent search. Understanding what agents can do for you, who they are, and the different types of agencies will ultimately make you that much more marketable to them.

Agents aren't gods. Really. But tell this to some writers and they'll openly scoff at you. These are usually the same writers who are apt to take rejections a little too personally. They're the writers who, after the rejections mount up, start to see agents as the enemy, an elite force blocking their way to *The New York Times* best-seller list. Suddenly, it's their pride that takes a beating, not their manuscript. Self-doubt creeps in. A wall of resentment goes up. "To hell with those agents," they declare, blind to the fact that selling writing is an agent's job.

The truth is, agents are human. Just like you and me. Only they're hardworking folks who pay their electric bills, day-care providers, and manicurists from the commissions they make on the sales of books and scripts. They have doubts, fears, feuds with landlords, ingrown toenails, failed diets, credit card debts, mothers who call them eight times a day, memoir-writing mothers seeking representation who call them eight times a day, complicated love affairs, and temporary crowns on particularly infected molars—and that's just a typical Monday.

nd out that there are
e truths, truths that

pe to make it in pub-
t, these truths apply

At one conference, a popular agent canceled her Saturday consults. When she arrived on Sunday, she looked like hell and soldiered through back-to-back appointments, trying to make up for the ones she missed. Later I learned that she had undergone chemotherapy the day before. Yes, agents get cancer too. In spite of spending the first half of her weekend puking and feeling like she'd been run over by a truck, she listened to writers pitch stories and tried her best to guide them to the knowledge they needed, maybe even to representation. She came to the conference that Sunday because she genuinely cared.

> **THINK OF AGENTS AS BOAT CAPTAINS WHO CAN GUIDE YOU THROUGH INDUSTRY WATERS. THEY'RE LIKE AN ARMY OF "CHARONS" FERRYING THE TALENTED ACROSS THE RIVER STYX.**

The Luxury Liners

Uber-agencies like William Morris Agency (WMA), Creative Artists Agency (CAA), United Talent Agency (UTA), International Creative Management (ICM), Endeavor Agency, Writer's House, Inc., and Janklow & Nesbit Associates come to mind. These are the transporters of the stars, the luxury liners of the agency world. They handle all areas of talent. Actors, screenwriters, directors, and authors. The giant agencies often specialize in "packaging"—working a deal where their actors, writers, and directors will all be rolled into one deal.

Are all agents and agencies here created equal? Hardly. These behemoths have their own internal pecking order. Top agents have astounding influence. The baby agents in these floating cities may lack the clout that comes with time and million-dollar deals, but they make up for it in attitude, resources, and long hours. Big agencies also have a high turnover rate, for agents and clients. With huge overhead costs, anyone not turning a profit is quickly tossed overboard. Many of these agencies require agents to bring in commissions equal to eight times their salary. (Example: If an agent makes five million dollars in gross sales, the agency's fifteen percent on five-mil equals $750,000. The agent's salary would be $93,750).

The Private Yachts

Many midsize agencies earn money by specializing. Some only handle writers. Some focus on genre. Book agencies like Levine Greenberg Literary Agency or Spectrum Literary Agency, both located in New York City, have agents that concentrate in particular areas such as nonfiction or romance. Other agencies, like Metropolitan Talent Agency and Paradigm Talent Agency in Los Angeles, are smaller versions of the luxury liners. Agents at midsize companies may be required to bring in four times their

nd out that there are
e truths, truths that

pe to make it in pub-
, these truths apply

salary in commissions. With solid industry connections, these agencies can be powerful in their own right.

The Dories

Sometimes called a "boutique agency," these operations are usually helmed by one or two agents. Agencies that handle the film side might have half a dozen interns and employees manning the phones. Rima Greer's L.A. Above the Line Agency, the Donald Maass Literary Agency, and the Doris Michaels Literary Agency are all great examples of highly productive agencies with many successful clients. Yet they don't have so many clients that they are unable to return a phone call. These utility boats are sturdy, long-term vessels. Boutique agencies and new writers can be a terrific match.

SO WHAT CAN AN AGENT DO FOR YOU?

An Agent Can …

- negotiate a sale
- escort your work to industry pros
- guide you toward a career (but ultimately you are responsible for producing product to sell)
- assist in making connections to other industry types

An Agent Can't …

- be your surrogate mother
- be your best buddy (no time)
- guarantee a sale
- guarantee a career

Remember, it's a business relationship!

ing intimida
ed by the se
ingly insur-
mountable v
of people wh
are already
the game? It
doesn't seem
fair. It's not.
The publishi
world is tou,
to crack. Wh
you are in th
early stages
getting peop
to notice you
talent, earni
a living
through you
creative
endeavors is
like trying t
climb Everes
with a roll o
tooth floss a
thumb tacks
for spikes.
There is no
room for am
teurs or the
equipped.
Those alread
mining wag
from this
extremely co
petitive indu
try don't wa

y self-worth. A reward for the long hours I'd logged on the chair, facing my monitor, pecking away at the keys. More than anything else in the world, I was determined to see my name print on the cover of a book. I was going to be a world-renowned author. My New York Times bestseller was just agent away. Surely, somebody would recognize my talent, spelling errors and all. This was quite the little fantasy I had playing between my ears. I did get published...eventu-

EMERGENCY
LIFE VESTS

Book authors, check to see that the agent who is offering you a contract is affiliated with the Association of Author Representatives (AAR). The AAR does not regulate commissions, fees, and services for agents, but they do provide a canon of ethics for their agent members. On the other hand, if an agent isn't an AAR member, don't assume that he or she isn't legit. Some agents choose not to join. The simple rule is: Real agents have real sales.

Visit www.aar-online.org.

Screenwriters, make sure your agent is a Writers Guild of America (WGA) signatory. As WGA signatories, agents must sign a book-sized agreement guaranteeing, among other things, set commission fees.

Visit www.wga.org.

first fifty pages." It was a validation of my self-worth. A reward for the long hours I'd logged on the chair, facing my monitor, pecking away at the keys.

nowing that
have a great
uscript, and
tead of leav-
ng the event
nspired, you
d up feeling
imidated by
e seemingly
urmountable
all of people
are already
he game? It
't seem fair.
ot. The pub-
ing world is
gh to crack.
n you are in
early stages
tting people
notice your
t, earning a
ng through
our creative
avors is like
ing to climb
erest with a
f tooth floss

SOME WRITERS GET DESPERATE

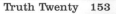

"We are not retreating—we are advancing in another direction."

~General Douglas MacArthur

Most working writers aren't born to Hollywood royalty and they aren't married to publishing executives. The majority of writers don't live in the "right" zip codes, associate with the "right" friends, or even have the "right" personalities. What most of them do have is a love of writing, perseverance, and good representation.

When you are first starting out, determination to be the best writer you can be may seem like the logical path to getting all the goodies life has to offer, but the grim truth of any creative endeavor is that there are no shortcuts to success. Sometimes the most talented fall to the wayside. And sometimes writers get desperate for a taste of success. So what do you do if you've already made all the "right" moves? For years?

You've attended the "right" classes, belonged to the "right" critique groups, and won the "right" contests, but you still don't have representation and are no closer to a publishing deal than you were five or ten years ago.

A lot of writers out there take matters into their own hands. This can be a good thing, or it can be a very bad thing, like forming a fake literary agency and representing yourself under a different name. I've known writers who have done this. Sometimes they involve friends. I advise against this ruse. Strongly. It's as silly as being your own defense lawyer in a murder trial.

Legit agents work hard at building relationships with editors, producers, and other professionals. They socialize with industry types over lunches and dinners. They read the books the editors are reading and acquiring so that they can better understand the tastes of each editor. Being an agent is hard work.

Another ploy used by writers and dishonest agents is false affiliations. Weaving a raft of lies, these people invent professional connections, friendships, and gossip about editors and producers. They name-drop legit agencies and famous people constantly. All to make it appear that they are finding success. They aren't. Real pros actually know the people behind the names that are being dropped. They don't have to crow about big-name associates. And they don't need to impress anybody.

The industry is very small. If there are six degrees of separation between any two people on earth, New York and Hollywood run on two degrees. Writers and agents who misrep-

el like you are on the
g in at your success-

you ever attended a
nce, book signing or

resent themselves will be exposed. If they are lucky, they will only be ignored.

Yet writers take creative and financial matters into their own hands all the time. They forge their own inroads and submit material on their own or through friends. They find and get paid for writing assignments on their own—without the help of an agent. Or they have an agent. A busy agent who has little time for them. Why wait around for success when they are perfectly capable of making things happen on their own?

"The fantasy days of agents being good angels are gone," says author and Pulitzer-nominated playwright Richard Vetere. An agent was once someone an artist needed to help plan the direction of their career. I say learn to make the moves your career needs "on your own. Artists have to take care of themselves. Any artist who is depending on an agent to run their career or life is naive."

> **OR AS SUN TZU SAID, "OPPORTUNITIES MULTIPLY AS THEY ARE SEIZED." PERHAPS IT'S TIME TO START MAKING YOUR OWN OPPORTUNITIES.**

MULTIPLY YOUR
OPPORTUNITIES

- **Organizations for writers.** Their newsletters and webzines advertise events that you should attend. From monthly confabs to cocktail parties and good old volunteer work, find opportunities for you.

- **Regional book fairs.** Many creative nonprofits, historical societies, and other cultural groups love to sponsor shindigs that feature authors. And most authors, shameless promoters that we are, love to attend.

- **Charity functions and social organizations.** Many people in the industry are also involved in other pursuits. Read the society page. Know who sponsors and attends what. Go to an auction (no need to bid). Sit in on a board meeting. March for something good. You can even consider becoming a volunteer.

- **Film school events.** Many are open to the public. A little research into a local film program can get you in the door and on your way to socializing with like-minded scribes.

fact, these truths apply everywhere and to every one because the industry a lot like the old high sch cafeteria. Especially to you new kid: Unfortunatel many writer who strive to make an impression o agents and e tors aren't aware of the social hierar chies and cu throat practices that ha existed for decades. The are oblivious the telltale signs that mark them a wannabes. Hence, the fo lowing Truth I can't guara tee that insic know-how w better your odds, but wit

- **Alumni newsletters.** Especially film school
  newsletters. These can give you access to movie
  premieres. Free. You don't have to be a graduate
  to RSVP (if you do, stretch the truth creatively
  and you might still get in). Many times aspiring
  filmmakers are anxious to fill the seats of their
  premieres or other events.

- **Author Web sites.** Send the author an e-mail.
  You would be surprised at how many authors
  answer their own e-mails. Don't be afraid to ask
  questions about the publishing industry.

- **State film board events.** Volunteer, sign up
  for mailing lists, go to the annual Christmas
  party. Check to see if your state has a govern-
  ment-sponsored film office.

- **Online.** There are plenty of chat boards. These
  are places where you can network with industry
  people at various levels.

- **Book-signing events.** Every city has them.
  Go. Introduce yourself. Schmooze if possible.

your odds, but without it... you may want to look for an easier occupation like nuclear astrophysics or Olympic water polo. Remember, this isn't a book on

xperiences,
ding a stint
vriting con-
ce coordina-
I met thou-
s of writers
like me, all
ng for their
. And I also
nd out that
are a series
core truths,
s that writ-
must learn,
pt and over-
come if they
e to make it
blishing. In
hese truths
pply every-
where and to
one because
ndustry is a
like the old
school cafe-
. Especially
u new kids.
fortunately,

TRUTH #21

MANY WRITERS ARE WORKING IN
THE STONE AGE

Ditch those old-fashioned editor and agent guide-books. The age of the e-query has arrived. "Although many of the printed directories are wonderful, their lead time can be a year or more and present only basic information in each listing," advises Ted Weinstein, who advertises for clients on the Internet. Filled with generalities, the old paper guides can't possibly keep up with what executives are looking for. This information changes on a monthly, weekly, and daily basis.

While the printed guides contain excellent inter-views, insights on crafting a proposal, and other snippets of information (you may want to keep one of these guides around for reference if you don't already have other more in-depth tomes), there is no need for you to part with hundreds of your hard-

"Queries by e-mail are great for writers and for agents. They save time, trees, and money for everyone."
~Ted Weinstein

earned dollars snail-mailing queries around the globe anymore. So let's skip another trip to the post office, save a wad of cash, and go directly to the Net. It's time to market from the comfort of home.

But a word of warning before we go: While e-queries are the new way of doing business, the Internet can be a huge time gobbler, and many writers have been lost to Web marketing. Some writers don't realize when it's time to stop, and there are no Web lifeguards to reel you back in from thousands of research hours. A good rule of thumb is to spend one hour of Net time for every two hours spent writing. After all, you can't call yourself a writer if you don't write.

So now it's your turn to practice. As you can see from the following examples, there are many different ways to spin a story. There are no rules for a perfect e-query, but by following e-query guidelines (see page 166) and practicing, you will get better.

What are you waiting for? Check out the following examples, then fire up your computer and get those fingers moving.

eling. All too well. I
f those writing con-

g and manuscript
y chest, I lined up

E-QUERY
EXAMPLES

Wrong:

Subject: Hi

Hi. Sorry to bother you. My name is Tish and I took a screenplay class last March and was hoping that maybe you could look at my stuff. It's not done yet but my instructor, Jonas Osgood (you went to film school with him, remember?), thinks my plot and characters are really great. Because it's about alien abduction I think it could be made for about ten million. Except for the part where the aliens land on a deep-sea oil rig. Anyway, I have a lot of interest in this story so you should probably read this real soon.

Bye,

Tish

PS – I won the community theater award for my portrayal of "Eve" in *Adam and Eve* in Bellingham, Vermont, in 1985 and since my script is based on my experiences I would love to star in the movie.

Right:

Subject: oil-rig disaster

Dear Mr. Edwards,

My script, an autobiographical thriller titled "To Mars and Back," is about being the sole survivor of a deep-sea oil-rig disaster. I was the only woman on a thirty-man crew, and I knew if I didn't confront the mysterious "accidents" that happened in the weeks leading up to June 3rd, 2001, I would be dead too.

I look forward to hearing from you.

Sincerely,

Tish Nygard

Ph: 000-0000

PS – My screenwriting mentor, Jonas Osgood (AFI class of 1998), sends his regards.

Right:

Subject: To Mars and Back

Dear Mr. Edwards,

My mentor, Jonas Osgood (you attended AFI with him) thought you might be interested in my screenplay "To Mars and Back." During the summer

of 2001, trapped on an oil rig in the Indian Ocean, thirty men perished under questionable circumstances. Only I came away to tell the story.

I look forward to hearing from you.

Tish Nygard

Wrong:

Subject: You'll regret deleting this e-mail

Hi – My name is Evan Arlen Vanderloo III. My grandfather was a dairy farmer. My father is a dairy farmer. Now, I'm carrying on the family tradition and I'm a dairy farmer too. My book is about the gulags of Siberia. Even though I have never traveled further east than Thornburg, Idaho, I have spent many hours in the library researching Siberia's penal system. If you become my agent, I know I will make you lots of money.

Evan

PS – I'm vegan and I hate cows.

Right:

Subject: Escape from Siberia

Dear Ms. Vernon,

After spending three years of research and working with a critique group, I finally feel that I am ready to market my novel. "Escape from Siberia" is a 400-page manuscript that follows Natalka Lubich, a Soviet Army defector who betrays her commissar father and receives a life sentence in Siberia's most dangerous gulag.

I hope that you will take a look.

Evan Vanderloo

Right:

Subject: runner-up prize

Dear Ms. Vernon,

Out of 2,600 entries, "Escape from Siberia," my novel about the Soviet Army's first imprisoned female defector, placed in the top ten of the Thornburg Literary Arts Festival.

I hope you will take a look.

Best, Evan Vanderloo

Right:

Subject: Thornburg Conference

Dear Pat Vernon,

ing intimidated by the seemingly insurmountable w of people whe are already in the game? It doesn't seem fair. It's not. The publishing world is tough to crack. Whe you are in th early stages getting peopl to notice you talent, earnin a living through you creative endeavors is like trying to climb Everest with a roll of tooth floss ar thumb tacks for spikes. There is no room for ama teurs or the i equipped. Those alread mining wage from this extremely co petitive indus try don't war

I was thrilled to see that you would be attending
the Thornburg Writing Conference. You were my
first choice for a consult. Unfortunately, your one-
on-ones booked quickly and I was not able to secure
a meeting. My novel, "Escape from Siberia," received
favorable comments from several editors. Two have
asked me to submit manuscripts. I am hoping you
will consider my work too.

Best regards,

Evan

Right:

Subject: Ashley Fort

Dear Ms. Vernon,

I'm sorry I missed speaking with you at the
Thornburg Conference. Ashley Fort, the conference
chairperson, suggested that my work might be
right for your agency.

About my manuscript: "Escape from Siberia" is a
fictionalized account of the Soviet Army's first female
defector and her against-all-odds flight to freedom.

Best regards,

Evan Vanderloo

THE FIVE PARTS OF AN E-QUERY

Before you type a single letter of the alphabet, let's discuss craft and what goes into the perfect e-query.

1. Subject line.

No threats, no clichés. Use your book title, a clever phrase that relates to the body of your e-mail, or, if a third party is involved, drop a name.

2. Introductions.

Address the agent in a professional manner. Show respect. Knowing their name—and spelling it correctly—shows you are paying attention.

3. Story.

Don't be a windbag. This is tricky territory, so come armed with a killer logline. You get only one sentence to describe your book or screenplay. If you are interesting, and I mean damn interesting, you may be able to get away with a couple of sentences.

ing intimidated by the seemingly insurmountable wa of people who are already in the game? It doesn't seem fair. It's not. The publishing world is tough to crack. Whe you are in the early stages of getting people to notice your talent, earning a living through your creative endeavors is like trying to climb Everest with a roll of tooth floss and thumb tacks for spikes. There is no room for amateurs or the ill equipped. Those already mining wages from this extremely com petitive indus try don't wan

apply every-
where and to
everyone
because the
industry is a
t like the old
high school
cafeteria.
Especially to
ou new kids.
nfortunately,
nany writers
who strive to
make an
npression on
ents and edi-
tors aren't
aware of the
social hierar-
hies and cut-
throat prac-
ces that have
existed for
ecades. They
e oblivious to
the telltale
signs that
nark them as
wannabes.
ence, the fol-
wing Truths.
can't guaran-
e that insider
now-how will
better your
ds, but with-
out it... you

4. Qualifications.

This is no place to tell them that you are "the next John Grisham." Your writing credits go here. Books, articles, poems published or e-published. Contest wins and honorable mentions. Don't have any? Go with your strong suit like professional connections or meeting them at a conference.

5. Graceful Exit

This is the big finish. If they haven't deleted your e-mail by now, you are in good shape. Thank them and sign off.

Now that your list of agents to e-mail is growing, what's next? Similar to snail-mail queries, writers need to know the rules before they hit "send."

Brevity Is Your Friend

NEVER write an e-query over five sentences. Short sentences. According to comedian Dennis Miller, our accelerated culture has given us the "attention spans of ferrets on a triple espresso." Get to your point. Quickly.

Avoid Vanity-Site Hell

Never ask them to check out your Web site. Not only do agents not care, they don't have time to peruse your Web page. Even if you've invented a cupcake recipe that cures cancer or have indie movie credits. Referring them to your site is the mark of an amateur.

Unfortunately, this is also a mistake that many professional writers continue to make. You may have written fifteen hundred published articles in the last ten years, but again, telling the agent to go to your Web site if they want further information is foolish. They won't. If they want to know more, let them hit "reply" and e-mail you directly.

eling. All too well. I
f those writing con-

g and manuscript
y chest, I lined up

Attachments Equal Rejection

NEVER send an attachment unless you are asked. When an agent asks to see your work via e-mail, only send exactly what they ask for. Furthermore, "accidentally" sending the first five hundred pages instead of the first five will only land you in the doghouse. Permanently. Screenwriters are rarely asked to send partial scripts via e-mail. Instead, you will be asked for a logline, synopsis, or full script.

Read Everything

This whole e-query business sometimes takes on the feeling of a lottery. It is. So treat it as one. Instead of spending money on each chance, you will be spending time. Those who want to "win" will pay careful attention to the small print.

There are two types of tickets your time can buy: One is the big agency with a decked-out Web site and query form. See www.inzide.com or www.levinegreenberg.com. The other is the independent who will contact you directly. For this type, see www.twliterary.com.

Whether you jump through hoops or dash off a quick five-liner, you must read the entire site before you query. Double- and triple-check the list of what they are looking for. There is nothing worse than sending off a pitch for a teen sitcom to an agent who handles civil war fiction, or querying a nonfiction agent with a prize-winning children's tale.

Capital Offense

Writing in all caps (uppercase) is sometimes referred to as "shouting." Many writers have used this method thinking that it will get the agent's attention. It will. In a negative way. USING ALL CAPS IS JUST PLAIN ANNOYING.

Form Letter Faux Pas

"Dear Agent"—the two words in the English language that make agents shudder. The "Dear Agent" form letter has been around for decades, only now it's morphed into a hybrid e-mail version that gets deleted just as quickly as the snail-mail version was once shredded.

To try and cut and paste your way to representation via mass-mailed missives shows a lack of respect. For yourself. And for the poor agent who receives this communication.

You may be able to cut and paste varying versions of your query to individual agents in separate e-mails, but make sure that you personalize each one as much as possible.

Here's an example. PublishersWeekly.com has an article on an agent who recently sold the memoir of a mathematician. Your project is about an algebra teacher who navigates the globe in a sailboat. In your e-mail, be sure to congratulate the agent on the mention in PW. Then be sure to draw a parallel between the agent's successful sale and your work. (Remember, ass kissers are loved! So pay attention.)

ling. All too well. I
f those writing con-

ig and manuscript
y chest, I lined up

Release Form Etiquette

Screenwriters who catch the attention of execs will usually be asked to sign a release form and send it along with their script. The release form will be sent to you as an attachment. If you cannot open the attachment (usually because the Hollywood company has newer software than yours), don't hound the exec for another format. Instead, drop by your local library or a Kinko's, sign onto one of their computers, and print the release there. Always print out a quality copy—this means no half-baked printer cartridges squeezing out their last drops of ink and no "recycled" paper (the other side of the page having doodles or an earlier draft of your synopsis). Cutting corners makes you look cheap and disrespectful.

"Did You Get My E-mail?"

Sending a follow-up e-mail asking the agent if they have read your first e-mail is a common mistake. If you haven't heard back in a few weeks, they are not interested. Accept it. Move on. E-queries are the second-to-last thing on agents' "To Do" lists. The last? Deal with all the damn mail that has stacked up on their desk over the past week.

Where to Start

A good place to begin your search for e-agents is Preditors & Editors at www.anotherealm.com/prededitors/pubagent.htm.

P&E is a comprehensive site that gives details on thousands of agencies. And it's FREE. Many of the listings provide agency Web sites. One click of the mouse and you are on your way.

There are also hundreds of writing Web sites and newsletters that list agents and agencies for book writers and screenwriters. Literaryagents.org and moviebytes.com both give scribes lots of information. But listings change often. Agencies come and go. Agents are promoted and demoted. Web sites fold. When you find a possible match for your work, an agent who takes an interest in your type of work or who has made sales in your genre, do a quick background check using a search engine such as Google. Working agents makes sales. And those sales are often catalogued on sites such as www.publishersmarketplace.com, a site that lists agent e-mail addresses and other contact info beside their recent successes.

eling. All too well. I
f those writing con-

ig and manuscript
y chest, I lined up

WINNERS DON'T
ALWAYS WIN

"Glory is fleeting, but obscurity is forever."
~Napoleon Bonaparte

If recognition, cash prizes, and bragging rights sound good to you, then chances are you've entered a writing contest. Sadly, contests are seldom a shortcut to signing with an agent or landing a coveted deal.

How do I know this? Because when I was starting out, I read books that told me I needed to enter contests to snare the attention of agents and I listened to instructors who harped on about the importance of establishing yourself by winning contests. So I entered contests. For a long time I didn't win squat, but as my writing skills improved I began winning. The best so far? Out of 3,400 entries my script took first place in comedy in a national screenwriting magazine contest. Not bad, but it didn't change anything. Sure, the prize money came in handy. The screenwriting software went to a friend, the

Waterman pen got hawked on eBay (give me a 99-cent gel roller any day), and the so-called coverage of a story that resembled my script got chucked.

There were no phone calls, few congratulations from fellow writers, and a handful of e-mails from producers who requested the script but, ultimately, did not even bother to send rejection letters or e-mails.

So contrary to the advice offered in almost every how-to-turn-pro book out there, contests wins will do little to launch you on the road to becoming a professional writer. And the next time an instructor stands in front of a class and spouts on about the importance of winning a contest, ask them how many contests they've won. If you can wring an answer out of them, it will likely be zilch.

Am I telling you not to enter contests? Heck no! Contest wins look good on a writing résumé—and they might even get an agent to read your work later on. So if you're going to enter, enter to win. Know what to enter, where you can win and how to muscle through the throng of entrants to grab for the gold.

Only Enter Your Best Work

Don't fool yourself into thinking that maybe the gods will smile on your second-rate effort and award you a prize anyway. Contest gods do not see Zen brilliance through the spelling mistakes. Ever.

experiences, includ-
writing conference

me, all longing for
and I also found out

They hit page three, see some minor inconsistency, and whammo, your work has bounced into the recycle bin. The gods have four thousand other entries to read, family coming for the weekend, and a poodle that needs to be picked up from the groomer. Only your best, several-times-proofed effort belongs on their desk.

Enter Appropriately

Every contest has a type of story that wins. Consistently. Mike Rich's *Finding Forrester* is a great example of the type of script that wins the Nicholl Fellowship. The Nicholl judges insist that all genres get equal consideration, but check to see how many teen slapsticks have won. Disney Fellowships aren't generally awarded to writers of gory, slasher stories. Romances à la Danielle Steele might pick up a prize or two in France, but they don't sweep the Pulitzers. Science fiction wins L. Ron Hubbard awards, bodice rippers don't. On that note, commercial fiction usually fares badly in literary competitions. But it does win contests elsewhere. Use your common sense, examine what has won in the past, then enter your best work.

Don't Go Broke

Many contests these days will accept your credit card number and happily process your entry fee. The costs add up fast if you are entering a lot of contests or sending multiple submissions. While most fees range from $30 to $60 per entry, some cost $100 or more. If entering contests causes you or your family a financial hardship, don't enter. And if you are putting the fee on your credit card because you don't have enough money in your checking account to cover that amount, reconsider.

Why am I being so brutal? Because I knew a woman from Tacoma, Washington, who entered and lost so many writing contests that she wound up being evicted from her apartment. Don't let that happen to you!

DO AN INTERNET SEARCH FOR FREE CONTESTS— ESPECIALLY THOSE SPONSORED BY PUBLISHING HOUSES AND STUDIOS.

Enter Smart

To help cut down on the number of eligible entries received and processed, there are groups that make entering their contests as difficult as possible. How does this help you? Let's put it this way. One state film board whittled their entries down to a mere 30 submissions this way. That makes your odds pretty good. So, with this in mind, think tiered judging, multiple self-addressed postcards, partial manuscripts, "official" mailed entry packets vs. downloadable or faxed entry forms, notarized entries, résumés and 1,500-word biographies. Film boards, fellowships, and festivals love to torture writers with these details.

experiences, includ-
a writing conference

TIRES

e me, all longing for
nd I also found out

DRINK

To enter smart, you must read everything in the submission guidelines. The smallest infraction of the rules and your work will hit the dumpster. These contests want your money, but rarely do they want to read your work. Readers cost money and the more entrants they bounce, the more money they keep.

Align Yourself With Winners

National corporations that sponsor contests (any contests, not just writing contests) stipulate that employees and family members of employees are not allowed to enter. Yet common sense and contest rules don't necessarily apply to many schools, low-circulation magazines, nonprofit organizations, literary agencies, writing conferences, production companies, and artist management companies. These groups can be rife with internal politics. Siblings of presidents win cash prizes and interns award each other top spots. I've seen it happen more than once. I've heard managers brag about all the money they take in from clueless writers, and it makes me angry.

IF YOUR GOAL IS TO BECOME A PROFESSIONAL WRITER, DON'T COMPETE WITH AMATEURS.

THE RIGHT
CONTESTS

Novelists, Nonfiction Writers, Poets, Short Story Writers, Essayists, and Memoirists:
Only enter established, well-known name-brand contests that have already launched professional writers. The right contests are sponsored by magazines and periodicals with national distribution. Fellowships and residencies should have name-brand recognition. Ditto for publisher-sponsored contests. Anything else and there's a very good chance you're throwing away your entry fee.

Screenwriters:
Nicholl, Heart of Austin, Chesterfield Film Company, and Disney. Occasionally studios, like Nickelodeon, will sponsor a talent search. Not all, but some of the writers who have won these contests found writing careers. If you're uncertain about the contest you'd like to enter, check with the Writers Guild of America. MAJOR contest winners may be eligible to join the WGA (whoo-hoo, this could mean health insurance, a mentorship program, and more). That said, only enter the major, WGA-approved contests. Sorry, most screenwriting magazine competitions don't cut it.

feel like you are on the outside looking at your successful, published friend and acquaintances? Have you ever attended a writing conference, book signing or literary gathering knowing that you have a great manuscript, and instead of leaving the event inspired, you wind up feeling intimidated by the seemingly insurmountable wall of people who are already in the game? It doesn't seem fair. It's not. The publishing world is tough to crack. When you are in the early stages getting peop

NOT ALL CRITIQUE GROUPS
ARE CRITIQUE GROUPS

It's easier to succeed with a group. Just ask Dorothy from *The Wizard of Oz*. She had Tin Man, Lion, Scarecrow, and a cute little dog to help her work things through. As with any ensemble endeavor, you need to have common or synergistic goals and members who want to cooperate in order to triumph in the publishing world.

Where will you find your yellow brick road? Online or in person, opportunities abound. Go to any bookstore bulletin board and there are usually half a dozen notices posted for writers seeking other writers for critique groups. Check the ads in writing-related periodicals. Cruise regional writing organizations and writing Web sites for groups. Wherever you are, there is a group looking for you. But not all critique groups are critique groups.

"Toto ... I have a feeling we're not in Kansas anymore."
~Dorothy, *The Wizard of Oz*

Some groups gather to write, socialize, or complain about the state of the publishing industry. I know of one group, getting up there in years, that plays Scrabble every two weeks. They haven't critiqued each other's work in years, but they still have dreams of writing the Great American Novel—despite the fact that they don't read words in anything less than a Scrabble-sized font.

There are also so-called critique groups that are organized by authors and instructors who charge for the service of being there. This is not a critique group. This is a class that offers critique. The leaders are a type of paid mentor. Yet it's still a group, they still critique, so what's the difference? Equality. In a critique group you get various points of view. Everyone has a chance to add his or her two cents. In a class, while other students may offer suggestions, the time is weighted to the teacher.

> **BEFORE YOU DIVE IN AND BEGIN YOUR SEARCH FOR A CRITIQUE GROUP, MAKE A LIST OF WHAT YOU WANT TO GET OUT OF THE EXPERIENCE ... LIKE GETTING PUBLISHED.**

There are many authors and writers who can help you craft your prose and make your manuscript the very best that it can be. But some critique group members are content with board games. Know what you want.

you have a great
d instead of leaving

ated by the seeming-
able wall of people

If you've been asked to join an established group (one that actually critiques), accept what is there. Groups that have been in existence for years are hard to come by. Bonds have been formed by longtime participants. If you are asked to submit a writing sample to one of these groups, be honored. If you're asked to join, be thrilled. And if you decide to form your own group, be selfish.

Good writers are usually good editors, so why not start there? But don't set your expectations too high either. Most critique groups aren't full of Pulitzer Prize winners. And if they are, and you haven't won any big literary awards, they may not want you. In the meantime ...

1. Look for people whose writing you can respect. Writers with agents, contacts, and writing expertise are ideal members.

2. Enthusiasm, dedication, and an eye for detail (proofreading) are valuable assets too. Chances are you will not find all these qualities in each one of your initiates, so you may need to choose one of the above-mentioned attributes per person.

3. Create a plan. Will members read pages out loud, then have the group offer comments? Or will the group read pages beforehand and concentrate on critique? Set a pattern.

4. Determine what's acceptable. Do you allow first-draft, single-spaced, stream-of-consciousness material to be reviewed? Is double-spaced, polished prose preferred? Or are you somewhere in between? The latter usually works

best as we all have our own styles, but depending on the skill of the writer, a first draft can be worthy of a critique. Have all members discuss what they are comfortable with. Come to an agreement on what constitutes readable work.

5. How much is too much? Some groups have a cap for submissions—like ten double-spaced pages. Others go by chapters. Since time is a valuable commodity, don't overwhelm your group with too much. It's better to do a good job critiquing ten pages than a poor job on a hundred.

6. To copy or not to copy? Some groups insist on photocopied handouts to all at the end of each meeting. Others zap chapters to one another via e-mail and Web-site posts. If you use the e-mail approach, make sure you set a deadline for chapters to be submitted. Nobody likes to receive twenty pages of single-spaced prose mere hours before the next meeting. A rushed critique is not fair to anyone. Whichever way you choose—handouts, e-mails, or posts—stick with it.

7. Look for balance. If you have an intermediate level overall, the addition of a wise old author may bring insights from the real world. The same can be said for the enthusiasm of a beginning writer who can often infuse an ongoing (stagnating) group with new life. If you are auditioning potential members, consider adding a novice writer who is committed to working on his or her project. This approach worked well for the

you have a great
d instead of leaving

ated by the seeming-
table wall of people

group I was in. As seasoned writers, we decided it was important to extend our knowledge to someone new. The joy we found in watching our baby writer grow up was a bimonthly reminder of just how far we had all come. Yes, believe it or not, most of us start out at the same terrible level.

I stunk too. Yep, I was awful. Miraculously, I was offered the privilege of joining an established duo, April and Tina. On the second and fourth Friday of every month, April, a hard-boiled mystery writer with several novels to her credit, and Tina, a ghoul writer, kicked my butt.

I wasn't very happy about it, but I came to every meeting anyway. Eventually I got better and I stopped tormenting April with my big, flowery sentences. I really stunk back then, but I think I turned out okay. (Thanks, April and Tina!)

DEVELOPING RHINO SKIN IS PART OF THE PROCESS OF BECOMING A WRITER.

The Etiquette of Giving Critique

- Never attack. If someone is writing a manifesto, your job is to aid them in making it the best manifesto ever written, no matter how much it creeps you out. If you have issues with religion, profanity, race, or nonvegetarians, keep them to yourself. It's about the writing, not you.

- Don't argue. It's pointless. This is not a debate. If you want others to consider your points at length, write them down and drop it. It's not your book.

- Never rewrite another member's work. It takes away from their experience. It taints their work with your voice.

- Never interrupt another member's critique. Got an urge to butt in? Button it, bite your lip, seal your mouth shut with masking tape. Interrupting is disrespectful, so wait your turn. If your turn has passed, make a note and talk with the author later. Privately.

- Write down your critique. A suggestion for a story twist may throw the author at the moment, but upon reflection, and reading your note later, it may be a useful tool.

- Always be constructive. "You're really talented, but I think it needs a 'page-one rewrite'" doesn't help anyone. Be specific. Show them you have read their work. Praise when praise is deserved, but never degrade another's work. Suggest stronger plotlines, better verbs, and clearer sentences at appropriate times.

- Keep it brief. Make your point. Quickly. Then move on.

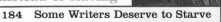

you have a great
d instead of leaving

ated by the seeming-
table wall of people

The Etiquette of Receiving Critique

- Keep your mouth shut. As much as possible. No defending. No arguing. No one is going to force you to implement any of the ideas put forth. Take what is useful and silently disregard what is not. You may answer questions if asked, but, as in Giving Critique, keep it brief.

- Take notes. It shows that you are paying attention.

- Thank them. These people read your work and thought about it. Thank them. And make it sound like you mean it. Later, after your hackles settle down, review the notes. If several people made the same comment, they might be right.

CRITIQUE GROUP
KILLERS

Some yellow brick roads lead down dark alleys where unsavory literary types lurk. These are the Critique Group Killers. While different personalities bring depth to a group, personality clashes bring depth with an anchor attached. If you want a group that makes you want to write, to improve, to succeed, avoid the following:

- **Drama Queens.** "Hello, spotlight." These writers were born ready for their close-up and will do anything to make sure the group revolves around them. If you want theater, buy a ticket.

- **Non-Writers.** You'll know them because they don't give out review pages. To anyone. These smooth operators have a great line and some fabulous stories. Don't allow them to talk you into letting them join, or remain, in your group.

- **Self-Professed Prolific Writers.** They'll give you tons of pages—pages that need vast amounts of work. Equitable is best. An eye for an eye, a page for a page.

feeling. All t
well. I was
once one of
those writing
conference
writers. You
know the typ
Heart pound-
ing and man
script clutche
to my chest,
lined up firin
squad-style
with two doz
other hopefu
and waited fe
my ten-minu
consult with
publishing
professional.
longed to hea
those magic
words, "Send
the first fifty
pages." It wa
a validation e
my self-wort
A reward for
the long hou
I'd logged on
the chair, fac
ing my moni
tor, pecking
away at the
keys. More
than anythir
else in the

- **Universal Know-It-Alls.** These are the writers who know absolutely everything in the universe. Expressing one's opinion is only half a benefit. The other half is being able to listen.

- **Deadly Silent Types.** They quietly bask in the attention. They absorb every word of your critique like a sponge. But when it's time for them to give a critique they come up with generic favorites like, "Um, that was nice," "I liked it," or "It's good." These writers haven't read your work, don't care to read your work, and have no intention of helping you or anyone else become a better writer. Lose 'em before their lackluster attitude sinks your group.

This was quite the little fantasy I had playing between my ears. I did get published...eventually. But getting from dreamland to reality, and actually seeing my name in print, was an adventure in dis-

w this feel-
All too well.
once one of
ose writing
erence writ-
. You know
type. Heart
unding and
manuscript
tched to my
t, I lined up
ring-squad-
le with two
dozen other
opefuls and
ited for my
minute con-
with a pub-
hing profes-
al. I longed
hear those
agic words,
end the first
ty pages." It
a validation
self-worth.
ward for the
ng hours I'd

WRITERS GET BITTER

"Don't worry, be happy."
~Bobby McFerrin

It's sad, but true. Writers lock themselves away in tiny rooms and peck at the keys until they can no longer communicate with other human beings except through written text messages. It's a pathetic existence and a bane to personal hygiene. Occasionally when under a deadline, it is acceptable to go "hermit," let the beard or armpit hair grow, eschew the shower, and pound out the words. It is also important to know when to cry "enough," bathe, and get out of the house.

I'm going to give you a little advice my mother would give me when I would lock myself away for days at a time working on my first novel. "Go out. Have a little fun. Meet people." Her message was clear: Be social.

While it's nice to hang out at the local bar and discuss pertinent issues like the minimum wage, sports scandals, and why microbrew beers taste better than mass-produced beverages, it's not helping your career. Why not combine your love of words and your social life?

You can start small. Many libraries have book discussion groups. Join a critique group. Enroll in your regional writers' organization. Go to a conference.

At first, finding and capitalizing on social opportunities seems as intimidating as getting your first bikini wax. It's humiliating. Trying to cultivate a suave and likable personality in a room full of people you don't know has your heart pumping double-time. It's impossible to relax. Your palms are sweating and your nervousness has made you tongue-tied.

I have two suggestions. One, get over yourself.

Everyone screws up. Laugh it off. At least then you are laughing with them. Two, if you can't function as yourself, choose another persona. When you are out with other writers, editors, or publishing professionals, picture the image of someone who would do well in this position. It may be that car salesman who talked you into buying a 1967 Plymouth Valiant as reliable transportation or the writer you see yourself being in the year 2030. Pick a persona, then act.

You may be feeling a bit screwed up about developing multiple personalities, but it can be a good thing. Besides, everyone has problems.

is a lot like the old
afeteria. Especially to

strive to make an
agents and editors

The publishing and film markets are tough places to turn deals (not to mention make friends). At all levels. Everyone is working an angle. Everyone wants something. Almost everyone already entrenched in these giant industries has their own goals, dreams, and insider cliques. It's a high-pressure, tactic-heavy battlefield. You have your agenda and they have theirs, but they were there first. And they already know the ropes, have a support group, and hear the industry gossip and secrets of the other players. They are in the game and you are not.

How can you sell something you love—your writing—to these people you can barely communicate with? Well, there's good news and bad news. The good news: There is always room for talented newcomers. Without newcomers, the same old faces make socializing dull. The bad news: There is always room for talented newcomers. Those grizzled old pros, the ones who were once newcomers themselves, are counting on you to fall flat on your face for their amusement. Like virgins sacrificed to pagan gods, a firepit reservation with your ego's name on it has been made. And there's no avoiding the flaming baptism.

It's not easy. You have to adjust. You have to push yourself out there. These are the pressures that make most writers bitter. And nobody wants to work or socialize with "the bitter." There is hope. Swallow your pride, put on a smile, and join the party. Be happy. Or at least fake it. And always know you aren't alone.

MY FLAMING
BAPTISMS

Although no one sets out to make themselves look bad, many do. Few people want to own up to their social screw-ups. Including me. But for your education and entertainment, I'll 'fess up. My own rocky start includes having a folder full of papers explode out of my hands and scatter over the floor ... just as a vice president of a major Hollywood studio asked me what my story was about. Embarrassed for both of us, he slunk off as I picked up the mess. It was my first introduction to someone famous. What can I say? At the time it felt like one of those goofy high school moments.

As a conference coordinator I've called agents by the wrong name. Repeatedly. Trust me, that is not good form and will not help you build a career.

And as a writer looking for a break, I made a huge faux pas at a party. Misjudging a Hollywood exec, I believed that he was parading me around as a respected, talented newcomer, not his latest applicant for a bedpost notch. Though others have made contacts this way, I would recommend against notching bedposts. It detracts from your professionalism.

experiences, including a stint as a wri ing conferen coordinator, met thousan of writers ju like me, all longing for their break. And I also found out th there are a series of core truths, truth that writers must learn, accept and overcome if they hope to make it in pr lishing. In fact, these truths apply everywhere and to every one because the industry a lot like the old high sch cafeteria. Especially to you new kid Unfortunatel many writer who strive to make an you have a great manuscript, and stead of leaving the event nspired, you wind up feeling intimidated by the seemingly insurmountable wall of ople who are lready in the ame? It doesn't seem fair. It's not. The publishing orld is tough crack. When ou are in the rly stages of etting people o notice your lent, earning a living hrough your creative endeavors is ike trying to limb Everest with a roll of oth floss and thumb tacks for spikes. There is no om for ama-

Fortunately, time dulls bad memories. It's important to accept that occasionally making a fool of oneself is just par for the course. Even the advanced err. It's human. And look on the bright side, if you tumble down the grand stairway for your entrance, humiliate yourself at dinner, or bolt the party in tears with your skirt tucked inside your pantyhose, hey, everyone will remember you. Okay, maybe that's not such a good thing. Let's hope your social debut will be a little less traumatic.

Through my
experiences,
ding a stint
writing con-
ce coordina-
, I met thou-
ds of writers
like me, all
ng for their
k. And I also
ind out that
are a series
core truths,
s that writ-
must learn,
pt and over-
come if they
e to make it
blishing. In
these truths
apply every-
where and to
one because
ndustry is a
like the old
school cafe-
a. Especially
ou new kids.

TRUTH #25

OVERNIGHT SUCCESS DOESN'T HAPPEN OVERNIGHT

Writers want everything. Now. You want an agent. You want to see your book in print. You want to host book signings with a line that goes out the bookstore doorway and around the block. A Pulitzer wouldn't hurt either. The only thing standing between you and your dreams is the realization that you don't have a clue how to get there.

For decades, conferences all across North America have served as a springboard for tens of thousands of aspiring authors and screenwriters to make the leap to full-time writing careers. Most conferences have at least one success story or "grand-prize winner," the writer who shows up with a rubber-band-bound manuscript and lands representation. On the spot. Just to be clear here, we all hate that person.

> "I love returning to a conference. I get to see how writers have progressed. I get to know them. It's the ones who keep coming back, keep learning, that have the best shot at publication."
> ~Donald Maass

But before we let the green-eyed jealousy monster get the best of us, let's take a look at the flip side of overnight success.

First off, there's no such thing. Not for writers. Writing requires time. Craft needs years to develop. And a good story sometimes takes a decade or more to find its way into print or to the screen. So adjust your mindset to the long haul right now and save yourself a lot of grief.

Second, instant gratification isn't always all it's cracked up to be. While I know of a handful of writers who have agreed to representation at a conference, only one actually signed a representation agreement before my eyes. She had a phenomenal, against-all-odds survival experience. And while her on-premises signing caused quite the sensation among attendees and certainly seemed like a dream come true at the time, this writer wound up getting taken advantage of by a fee-charging agent.

There was a happy-ever-after ending. Later. She eventually signed with a real agent who went on to sell her memoir to a major Canadian publisher.

On that note, the paperwork usually comes later too. Most agents like to read an author's work before they commit, unless the story is incredibly outstanding or original. If you've done your research, checked to see if your targeted agents are affiliated with the Association of Author's Representatives or signatories to the Writers Guild of America, you won't have a similar problem.

my self-worth. A
he long hours I'd
ng away at the keys.
rything else in the

WRITING CONFERENCE CHECKLIST

- **Do your research.**

  Read the brochure. Are there speakers you wish to talk with? Are there agents you want to approach? What about editors? Make a list. Now research that list. Get on the Internet. Google them. Read old articles about them. Find their backgrounds, affiliations, and interests. What have they sold? Who do they represent? Research their clients. Know everything you can about the people you want to connect with.

- **Set attainable goals.**

  If there are thirty-five agents and editors at the conference, don't tell yourself that you MUST pitch to each and every one of them or else your weekend will be a waste. You have not failed if only one agent requests pages. One is a success. Also, contact the conference coordinators to see who might be right for your work. They invited these people. They should know.

- **Know your work will find its audience.**
  Eventually. You must believe this. In the weeks and days before the conference, start building up your ego. It's okay to love your work and yourself. Just don't get too effusive. Even if you are only able have a handful of consults, or you only have one consult, there are other conferences. More queries to write. This is one step in a big plan.

- **Sign up for classes.**
  Ones that interest you. Don't plan to devote all your time toward consults and pitching. Get out there. I do. Yes, even people who have written books and organized conferences still have a thing or two to learn. You do too.

- **Don't take yourself too seriously.**
  This is hard to do after all the time and energy you've taken to prepare for this event. You want to do well. But with all that pressure on you, you may just explode. Take the pressure off. You've done the research. You have your plan. Now just tell yourself that this is a test run. There are a hundred other conferences. This one is just practice. Relax.

those magic words, "Send the first fifty pages." It was a validation my self-worth A reward for the long hou I'd logged or the chair, fac ing my moni tor, pecking away at the keys. More than anythir else in the world, I was determined t see my name in print on th cover of a book. I was going to be a world-renowned author. My New York Times best-seller was ju an agent awa Surely, some body would recognize my talent, spelli errors and a This was qu the little fan

like me, all
longing for
their break.
And I also
ound out that
there are a
series of core
ruths, truths
that writers
must learn,
accept and
overcome if
they hope to
ake it in pub-
lishing. In
fact, these
truths apply
everywhere
and to every-
one because
he industry is
a lot like the
old high
school cafete-
ia. Especially
to you new
kids.
nfortunately,
many writers
who strive to
make an
mpression on
ents and edi-
tors aren't
aware of the
social hierar-
hies and cut-

- **Be prepared to have fun.**

   These events are circuses. And life under the
   big top is fun, right? Pack notebooks to jot down
   ideas for future character development. Believe
   me, you will meet lots of characters. Consider
   after-hours parties or a drink in the hotel bar.
   Be prepared to get out there and socialize. There
   are breakfasts, lunches, and banquets. Sign up.
   You never know who you will be sitting next to.
   Also circulate. Don't settle in with a nice, safe
   clique. You're going there to meet as many people as you can: fellow attendees, volunteers, and
   the industry pros.

their time on newcomers. And if you do show promise, established authors don't want younger or more
talented scribes vying for jobs and contacts on their

ow this feel-
All too well.
once one of
nose writing
erence writ-
s. You know
type. Heart
unding and
manuscript
tched to my
t, I lined up
ring-squad-
yle with two
dozen other
opefuls and
aited for my
minute con-
with a pub-
hing profes-
al. I longed
o hear those
nagic words,
end the first
ty pages." It
a validation
y self-worth.
ward for the
ng hours I'd

WRITING CONFERENCES
COST BUCKS

Shawguides.com lists more than 1,500 annual writing conferences in North America. There are writing organizations for almost every type of writer out there. The Romance Writers of America holds annual gatherings all over the United States. Hundreds attend events for science-fiction scribes. Screenwriters have over a dozen conferences devoted to improving their craft and marketing their work to producers. Ditto for mystery writers and children's authors. On top of that, regional conferences serve up a wide array of fiction and nonfiction programs.

All these conferences have two things in common. One, a lot of writers pass through the doors of each event. My favorite conference had 826 registered attendees. Add in agents, editors, speakers, staff, and volunteers and that number topped one

"Obstacles are those frightful things you see when you take your eyes off the goal."
~Henry Ford

thousand. My second favorite conference had a grand total of 787 writers sharing stories, learning craft, and pitching projects. With all these people coming together under one roof with the same goals in mind, possibilities abound.

The second thing that these events have in common is that they all cost money to attend. Usually several hundred dollars. Sometimes more. Add in transportation, hotel bills, banquet tickets, consult fees, and a trip to the onsite bookseller, and you could be looking at a credit card bill of one thousand dollars or more.

For the most part, conferences are a good value. Still, not everyone is able to afford the cost of admission. And then there are some folks who just want to save a few bucks. That's understandable.

Eight Ways to Save Money

1. If you can't afford a full conference package, consider attending a conference that allows you to sign up for one day only. With a little planning you may be able to condense your consults and classes into a short period of time.

2. Only attend the banquet. Some organizations will allow you to buy a separate ticket for evening social events. If not, try to connect with someone who is attending the conference to see if they'll purchase an extra ticket on your behalf. (You'll pay them back, of course.) Arrive early. Schmooze.

When you are in the
f getting people to

reative endeavors is
climb Everest with a

3. Read the brochures and conference Web sites. There is a conference for every need and budget.

4. If you're traveling and need to cut costs, some conferences offer a room share program.

5. If you don't stay on site, you may be able to save even more money. Check out nearby hotels and hostels for lower room rates. But be sure to consider the travel time between the conference location and your discounted digs.

6. Be prepared to spend a little more than you anticipated. Opportunities can pop up at the most unexpected times. There might be an opening in a previously sold-out master class. Consultation spots often become available when other attendees cancel. And who knows, you might be invited to go out on the town with a group of authors and their agents. All of the above have happened. To me. To fellow writers I know. Pay attention and pad your budget so that you won't have to decline a last-minute possibility because you don't have the funds.

SIGN UP EARLY. IT IS THE EASIEST WAY TO SAVE A SIGNIFICANT AMOUNT OF MONEY. ALMOST ALL CONFERENCES OFFER EARLY-BIRD DISCOUNTS.

7. Whatever you do, don't crash a conference. These events cost organizers tens of thousands of dollars. Sometimes over a hundred thousand. They are not the cash cows you might think they are.

   That said, years ago I crashed a conference. In Seattle. And I got tossed out on my butt and asked never to return. The upside of this situation was that in the lobby I got to speak with the one agent I was dying to meet. Better yet, she requested the first fifty pages of my project. As the odds would have it, nothing happened there.

   The real downside of my "crashing" experience was karmic retribution. I became a conference coordinator.

8. Finally, if you're really strapped for cash, volunteer!

. When you are in the
of getting people to

creative endeavors is
climb Everest with a

VOLUNTEER
PROTOCOL

Ever thought about volunteering? It's a great way to see how a conference works, share your time and skills—and get free access to classes, agents, and even editors.

Unfortunately, some volunteers expand those opportunities too far. At one conference, a volunteer driver loaded her van full of tired agents and editors who were expecting to be driven downtown. In order to spend as much time as possible with them and pitch her story in great detail, the driver took a scenic route. A very scenic route. Instead of a twenty-minute commute west, she drove east. By the time the agents realized what was going on, they were over an hour from downtown!

How do I know this? My agent was in that van.

Kidnapping the industry pros is never a good way to get their attention. If you get the chance to volunteer, consider the following:

- Larger conferences require volunteers to sign up six to eight months in advance.

elling. All too well. I was once one of those writing conference writers. You know the type. Heart pounding and manuscript clutched to my chest, I lied up firing-squad-style with two dozen other hopefuls and waited for my ten-minute consult with a publishing professional. I longed to hear those magic words, "Send the first fifty pages." It was validation of my self-worth. A reward for the long hours I'd logged on the chair, facing my monitor, pecking away at the keys. More than anything else in the

- Many nonprofit organizations have special allowances for volunteers who are disabled or on limited retirement incomes.

- All volunteers should be prepared to work hard. Don't worry. You'll have fun and meet lots of people. Just don't expect to have a high energy level at the end of the day.

- If you get the chance to strike up a conversation with an editor or agent, and they inquire about your work, be brief.

- Or better yet, ask if you could send them an e-mail or query letter with a short description of your project.

- Discuss common interests, the state of the widget industry, anything but your project. You are laying groundwork here. When you do contact them after the conference, remind them of the drive to the airport or the time you spent getting a restaurant reservation for them. Chances are they will read your work.

- And never, never, never kidnap them.

world is toug
to crack. Wh
you are in th
early stages
getting peop.
to notice you
talent, earnin
a living
through you
creative
endeavors is
like trying to
climb Everes
with a roll of
tooth floss an
thumb tacks
for spikes.
There is no
room for ama
teurs or the i
equipped.
Those alread
mining wage
from this
extremely co
petitive indu.
try don't war
to waste thei
time on new-
comers. And
you do show
promise, esta
lished author
don't want
younger or
more talente
scribes vying

SEX HAPPENS

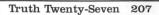

"That's a nice little nothing you're almost wearing."
~James Bond

It's inevitable. Conference sex. Hundreds of men and women, under stress, laying out their hopes and dreams ... the conference staff might as well be pumping pheromones through the ventilation system. While love and lust have blossomed at many consult tables and cocktail parties, be aware that there is a pecking order when it comes to this sort of interaction. "Putting out" may get you in, but chances are you will not get ahead.

There is a moral code of commandments to cover these couplings:

1. Agents, editors, entertainment lawyers, managers, or producers shall not have sexual relations with unpublished, unrepresented writers.

2. Agents, editors, and other industry pros may all happily, and constantly, bed one another.

3. Agents shall not have sex with another agent's client. It's poaching at its lowest form.

4. Authors, published and unpublished, may boink away on each other at any time.

This is the code that is ignored by many participants much of the time. Every conference has dozens of scandals. And it's not just the men taking advantage of the women. At the last conference I organized, one prominent female agent had a meeting with an attractive male writer, then, later, simply had him in her room. Sex happens. But this isn't a who's who of who's doing who.

THE POINT IS: BE WARY.

If you are ready to do anything (or anyone) to make your career happen, there will always be people with power available to make some tempting offers. One woman I know was seduced by a famous author and his promise to introduce her to his big-time editor. The sex happened. The introduction never did. He went home to his wife and kids and she got her heart and hopes broken. Or at least crippled. Later, I heard through the grapevine that she had persevered and a local press had picked up her nonfiction book for publication, no thanks to the famous author.

There are also those sexual predatory types among us who stalk those who have the power to give them what they want, be

experiences, includ-
a writing conference

e me, all longing for
nd I also found out

it a book contract or movie deal. This happens a lot in Hollywood. Tales of the casting couch abound for a reason. It also happens anywhere that writers gather with industry power players. Places like conferences. I'm just saying, sex happens. More often than you think.

I don't want to preach morality or abstinence. Those are your choices. I'm simply warning you that if you do use sexual favors as a way to climb the ladder, you will probably be more disappointed if your phone calls aren't returned, or your manuscript comes back unread with a form letter, than those writers who depended on their writing alone.

There is a bright side to these fornication issues. You don't have to have sex to be social. Though there are codes for your party behavior, too.

PARTY
PROTOCOL

- Organized conference events abound. There are banquet dinners, film screenings, schmooze-athons. The key to your actions here are simple. Anything you would not do at your sister's wedding, you should not do here.

- Cocktail hours can yield marvelous opportunities. If there is an organized cocktail hour but it is by invitation only, don't crash. There will be other times and places to socialize. On the other hand, it never hurts to politely ask if you can join. Or failing that, if you recognize someone in the room, you might bamboozle the door guard into letting you enter for a quick chat. But never overstay your welcome.

- If you are invited to a private cocktail hour, never invite extra guests unless you have cleared it with the host or hostess. If you break this rule, you may find a sharp decline in future invitations.

- If there isn't a cocktail hour at your event, invent one. After classes, meet for drinks in the hotel lounge. Before a keynote speech is an

experiences, including a stint as a writing conference coordinator, I met thousands of writers just like me, all longing for their break. And I also found out that there are a series of core truths, truths that writers must learn, accept and overcome if they hope to make it in publishing. In fact, these truths apply everywhere and to everyone because the industry a lot like the old high school cafeteria. Especially to you new kids. Unfortunately many writers who strive to make an

Times best-
seller was just
n agent away.
Surely, some-
body would
recognize my
alent, spelling
errors and all.
This was quite
he little fanta-
sy I had play-
ing between
my ears. I did
get pub-
shed...eventu-
ally. But get-
ting from
dreamland to
reality, and
ctually seeing
my name in
print, was an
adventure in
discovering
he customs of
a foreign land
publishing). I
arned to keep
my network-
g radar on at
all times (you
never know
who you will
meet) and,
most of all,
face the fact
nat the moun-

excellent time too. Post-banquet parties are great
for night owls. Camaraderie is GOOD. Get out
there and mingle.

- If you host a gathering in your room, be festive.
Think music, tablecloths, flowers, snacks, and
drinks. Be the gracious master of ceremonies.
While you're at it, don't go overboard and invite
so many people that you're in violation of the fire
codes. On the other hand, make sure there are
plenty of chatty types who will make the conversations flow. Also, don't let your party get out of
hand. Have a time limit. Let everyone know you
need your beauty sleep and wrap things up at a
decent hour.

- Always use common sense. Whether you are the
host or invitee, this isn't your sister's wedding.
Your new friends are, ultimately, strangers.
So play safe.

tasy I had playing between my ears. I did get published...eventually. But getting from dreamland to reality, and actually seeing my name in print, was an

w this feel-
ll too well.
once one of
ose writing
rence writ-
. You know
type. Heart
unding and
manuscript
ched to my
, I lined up
ring-squad-
le with two
lozen other
opefuls and
ited for my
ninute con-
with a pub-
ing profes-
al. I longed
hear those
agic words,
nd the first
y pages." It
a validation
self-worth.
vard for the
g hours I'd

CONSULTS ARE NOT AN OLYMPIC SPORT

Conference consults are great. These are your one-on-one appointments to talk to or pitch the pros. They can also be exhausting.

Find out how many consults are included in your admission fee, if you can sign up for additional consults, and for how much. I know of one woman who signed up for our regional conference just for the consults. She booked every consult offered, skipped the classes, and haunted the consult sign-up desk to buy any no-show slots.

She also loitered outside the exit door of the consult room and politely asked exiting agents if they would consider her material. While most attendees had four consults, this woman racked up an amazing thirteen "send me your work" opportunities. She talked to almost every agent and editor at the conference. Is she famous now? Well, no. You also have to have something they want to buy.

Unfortunately, when it comes to consults, inside or outside the official pitch room, some attendees get desperate. And it's not pretty. They treat consults like an Olympic sport. Every appointment seized, agent "nailed," editor pitched, and manager stalked is another gold medal on their personal tally sheet. No wonder that these publishing and film pros—regular folks Monday through Friday—suddenly feel like rock stars on conference weekends. Mobbed by writers at lunch, in the hall, and during cocktail hour, they can't take three consecutive steps without being asked a question, pitched a story, or invited for dinner. Some groupies even go to extremes, shadowing their "pitch target" to the elevator and throwing their bodies into the path of closing metal doors. Yikes! Why not use a more sensible approach?

rious to the telltale
them as wannabes.

insider know-how
r odds, but without

feeling. All too
well. I was
once one of
those writing
conference
writers. You
know the type.
Heart pound-
ing and manu-
script clutched
to my chest, I
lined up firing-
squad-style
with two dozen
other hopefuls
and waited for
my ten-minute
consult with a
publishing
professional. I
longed to hear
those magic
words, "Send
the first fifty
pages." It was
a validation of
my self-worth.
A reward for
the long hours
I'd logged on
the chair, fac-
ing my moni-
tor, pecking
away at the
keys. More
than anything
else in the

CONVERSATION
PROTOCOL

- Do not wait your turn, inches away, while the agent
  is speaking to someone else. It's rude. It's creepy.
  And stalkers are never asked to submit material.

- Do not nonchalantly follow an agent to the bathroom. Stalls are not confessionals. Urinals are not
  meant for impromptu pitching. Again, creepy.

- Do jockey for a spot at their banquet table, but don't
  be obvious about it.

- If your efforts are completely washing out, talk
  to a member of the conference staff. Often they can
  arrange an introduction. As a conference coordinator
  I've done this dozens of times. Since I already know
  the roster of agents and editors, it's easy to escort
  someone up to the agent and say, "By the way, I'd
  like you to meet so-and-so." Once introduced, keep
  your conversation brief.

- Remember, your goal is to start a conversation, not
  necessarily to pitch your product. You can always
  pitch or query later, after the conference. The goal
  is to begin building relationships.

Consult Etiquette

You booked your one-on-one appointments months in advance. You've practiced your pitch, polished your shoes, and prepared yourself for any questions they might ask. Now what?

First, don't be nervous. I know, easier said than done. If you are truly nervous, knees shaking, palms sweating, tell the agent or editor you are nervous. They will understand. One attendee at a recent conference was so tongue-tied that each time he sat down for a consult he would freeze. Solid. Practicing his pitch with a professional writer didn't help much, but he was able to write down his pitch on the back of an envelope. Five sentences. For his next consult, he read the sentences aloud and the agent said, "Send."

Hopefully, you'll be a little more relaxed than that when you sit down and introduce yourself. The correct way to approach a consult is calmly. Be a Zen Pitch Master.

- Ask your host if he is enjoying the conference. A little chitchat can go a long way.

- Mention any credentials you may have. Briefly!

- Tell them the title of your project.

- Label it (thriller, romance, nonfiction, etc.).

- Proceed calmly into your short pitch.

- Leave enough time for them to ask questions.

vious to the telltale
k them as wannabes.

insider know-how
r odds, but without

- Let the agent lead the post-pitch conversation.

- Cut yourself some slack. If you mess up, move on. We all bomb from time to time.

- If you encounter a producer who is talking on his cell phone while you are trying to pitch, or an agent who is counting ceiling tiles instead of listening to you, their rudeness is not your problem. Tell the conference staff and ask for a refund or another complimentary consult.

- Don't focus on industry professionals only. If you get the chance, speak with instructors, organizers, and members of the organization's board of directors. You will be pleasantly surprised at how much you will learn in a short conversation.

- Meet as many fellow attendees as possible. Conferences are famous for long lines—for lunch, for the bathroom, for extra consults, for buying anything. Use this time to your advantage. Find out as much as possible about your fellow attendees. Your next mentor, critique group, or writing retreat could be the result.

- If you're new to pitching, avoid consult burnout. Don't schedule four back-to-back consults. Give yourself time to reflect after each consult.

- Never overstay your welcome. If the agent says "send," good for you. Get their contact info and get out. Don't stick around and give them reasons to rescind their offer. Once an agent commits to reading your pages, that's enough. You can go. Bye-bye.

- Allow them to decline. If an agent says, "No, thank you, it's not for me," don't try to convince them it is. If you still have time on the clock, you may ask questions about the industry or markets. When your time is up, thank the agent for their time and leave gracefully.

eing. All too
well. I was
once one of
those writing
conference
writers. You
now the type.
Heart pound-
1g and manu-
cript clutched
to my chest, I
1ed up firing-
squad-style
ith two dozen
ther hopefuls
nd waited for
1y ten-minute
onsult with a
publishing
professional. I
onged to hear
those magic
words, "Send
the first fifty
pages." It was
. validation of
1y self-worth.
A reward for
1e long hours
I'd logged on
the chair, fac-
ing my moni-
tor, pecking
away at the
keys. More
han anything
else in the

NO BOOK? NO PROBLEM!
(IF YOU HAVE A PLATFORM)

In this day and age, being an author is not always
about toiling away in solitude and liberating ink to
paper. Being an author can be about Web presence,
promotions, and name-brand recognition. Publishers,
in addition to buying manuscripts, also buy people.
People who promote the hell out of ideas, concepts,
and products via public presence. These savvy types
are marketable commodities. Think Bill O'Reilly,
President Clinton, Jimmy Buffet, and Deepak Chopra.
Think Oprah Winfrey, Oprah Winfrey's fitness guru,
and Oprah Winfrey's personal chef. You get the idea.
But you don't have to be famous or linked or someone
famous to be a marketable commodity.

Tens of thousands of speakers and would-be
authors are out there trying to improve, combat, or
cure politics, waistlines, fly-fishing, wardrobes, etc.
They are carving out names for themselves in the
marketplace by building a platform.

Platform \ plat~form \ noun

1: a raised flooring or stage for speakers

2: a declaration of principles on which a
   group stands

3: your ability to reach prospective buyers of your
   product—this means media presence, speaking
   gigs, anything and everything that brings public recognition of your name and writing

Agents and publishers love a platform.
It equals sales.

feel like you
are on the ou
side looking
at your suc-
cessful, pub-
lished friend
and acquain-
tances? Have
you ever
attended a
writing confe
ence, book
signing or lit
erary gather
ing knowing
that you hav
a great manu
script, and
instead of lea
ing the even
inspired, you
wind up feel-
ing intimida
ed by the see
ingly insur-
mountable w
of people wh
are already i
the game? It
doesn't seem
fair. It's not.
The publishi
world is toug
to crack. Wh
you are in th
early stages
getting peop

TRUTH #29

NOT ALL HOLIDAY GIFTS
ARE WELCOME

You've been expanding your knowledge and contacts through classes and socializing with peers. Perhaps you've attended a conference and developed a circle of writers who have aspirations similar to yours. And then December rolls around.

Critique groups take a few weeks off to celebrate Christmas and Hanukkah with friends and family, moviemaking and publishing slow to a crawl, and you're scrambling to complete your card and gift lists. On top of that, party season has begun and you're still figuring out how to lose those pesky ten pounds that you put on last Christmas. But there's nothing like the holidays: a time of reflection, appreciation of our loved ones, and finding our moral centers. It's also one big, fat networking opportunity.

Ho-Ho-Who?

Slow up there, Santa. Before you hustle off to the mall, the post office, or speed-dial your UPS dispatch, let's discuss WHO you might want to send something to during this season of giving.

At the top of your list should be anyone who has considered your work over the last year or has asked to see future projects.

Hmmmm. Is your list looking a tad anorexic? No problem. Consider the six degrees of separation theory. Scribble down the names of anyone you met and exchanged contact info with at book signings, literary events, and conferences. Now add on the teachers of the writing classes you've attended. And not just this year's workshops—jot down the names of instructors going back a couple of years. Sometimes those "career launching" people aren't the ones you know directly, but the ones someone else knows. Remind everyone you're still here.

Holiday Cheer

Your list has probably swollen up toward a hundred. Now let's take a look at WHAT to send. How about a partridge in a pear tree (100 percent Belgian chocolate, of course) for that Hollywood producer who thought your Twelve Days of Christmas thriller was a "little too low budget" for his company? Or a giant coffee mug for the teacher who loved your barista-in-love romance, but thought it needed another polish? Maybe funny photos of you, au naturel, with a Santa hat and a manuscript strategically placed to that

show promise, estab-
don't want younger

ts on their turf. The
closed to you. The

good-looking editor who requested your book at the conference, but still hasn't returned your calls? As usual, we're all a little befuddled over who gets what.

Here's the easy answer. Skip the clever gifts and go with a card. A tasteful greeting card is always in good form. Make it warm. Make it thoughtful. Use your wit sparingly.

Isn't that easy? No gifts!

To give a gift runs the risk of insinuating they owe you a favor, a read, a critique, an acceptance. And they don't owe you anything. Furthermore, sending a gift takes away from you. When you speak to these people in the new year, the focus should be on your writing, not the gift you sent an agent, editor, or producer. Besides, isn't everyone uncomfortable with acquaintances who lavish gifts? Establish your connections first.

E-Greetings

If you only have e-mail addresses for some of your contacts, go ahead, send your well wishes via the Net. Skip e-greeting cards, humorous attachments, or fancy fonts. Not everyone has the time to download pictures and jingles, and even fewer have a sense of humor during the holidays. Pare your yuletide wishes down to a simple black and white twelve-point text message. Believe me, your friends and associates will recall your message fondly when some bozo sends them a twelve-minute musical card featuring animated reindeer.

Rules to Sleigh By

You're doing this to network, so before you get to work licking stamps and addressing envelopes, keep in mind the following guidelines:

- Never pitch your project or give them a running account of where your manuscript stands. The holiday season is about giving, not angling to get a read out of an already busy reader or editor. This postal exercise is all about staying in touch, building relationships.

- Do not include the standard photocopied yuletide newsletters that painfully detail your family vacation to Yellowstone Park and Fido's latest litter of puppies.

- No photos. Ever. "But there were hundreds of people at the conference, how will they know who I am if I don't send a picture?" Let them remember you by your unforgettable words. Your talent. The way you craft the English language that makes them weak at the knees.

- There is one gift exception—and it has nothing to do with Christmas. If an agent makes a first sale for you, a bottle of champagne is not unheard of. If your book comes out and is greeted with lavish praise by the critics, you may want to send flowers to that editor who forced you through twelve rewrites.

show promise, estab-
don't want younger

cts on their turf. The
closed to you. The

For right now, the best gift you can give yourself and others is your writing. Your fabulous writing. Nothing makes an agent happier than receiving a requested, well-crafted original manuscript that flows with style and professionalism.

So remember, the holiday season is an excellent time to be renewing acquaintances, laying some groundwork for the year ahead, and sending out sincere wishes of publishing and movie-making success to all.

see my name in print on the cover of a book. I was going to be a world-renowned author. My New York Times bestseller was just an agent away. Surely,

ve you ever
nded a writ-
conference,
signing or
rary gather-
ng knowing
you have a
great manu-
script, and
tead of leav-
ng the event
spired, you
d up feeling
imidated by
e seemingly
urmountable
all of people
are already
he game? It
't seem fair.
ot. The pub-
ing world is
gh to crack.
n you are in
early stages
tting people
notice your
t, earning a

THE WRITING IS
NEVER DONE

"A poem is never finished, only abandoned."
~Paul Valery

We all want to see our literary dreams realized. It's a long road from "Gee, I have an idea" to holding the book in your hand. There are many points along this path; many times you may feel like you're done … but you're not.

Okay, so you've written your manuscript, had friends and colleagues critique it, reworked it, had a proofing party to get the typos out, and know that this is the absolute best that this project can be. Ever. It's done.

Now all you have to do is find someone who can locate a buyer for it. You use your pitch to contact agents online and at conferences. You send the pages out as requested. Eventually, an agent signs you on as a client. And now, after careful professional consideration, your representation wants you to rewrite your masterpiece and make it more commercial.

YES, YOU HAVE TO REWRITE OR GO BACK A STEP AND START AGAIN.

But why should you take your agent's advice when you know you have written a masterpiece? Because they know the market. They know what is selling. They read thousands of manuscripts. You don't argue with your doctor, do you? Don't argue with your agent (though if you want a second opinion, get it before you sign the contracts).

After you've rewritten your book for your agent, it goes out into the world. Sometimes it will be sent out to one editor at a time. Sometimes it will go to a dozen publishers at once. It's exciting as comments and rejections come in. Hopefully an offer follows. If an offer does come in, then it's over. The book has sold. You're finally done.

Wrong.

Now the acquiring editor has notes. General notes to help your book fit into their overall lineup and publishing strategy.

You rewrite.

Next, a second group climbs onboard. Some are editors who specialize in grammar or content. There are people who look at the layout of the book. There is still more advice from the marketing department (selling a book begins long before it actually gets published). Your job is to make everyone happy. And rewrite, rewrite, rewrite.

y to you new kids,
many writers who

itors aren't aware of
irchies and cutthroat

A friend of mine who worked with a particularly tumultuous new imprint of a major publisher went through six editors before her book went to press. Six! While everyone on the team was working toward the same goal, each editor had his or her own agenda. She later told me that once you hold the book in your hand, you forget about the long hours it took to get there and the battles waged over cut paragraphs and chapters.

So moving on, after you rewrite, rewrite, rewrite, you reach the next stage. Galleys. This is what the book will look like once it's published. And this is your last chance to make changes.

For my last book I had a galley party where I invited my most trusted and gifted proofreaders. I abused their talents horribly with the promise of endless margaritas afterward (never during). It was amazing how many typos were still in the text.

When you approve the galleys, you are completely, 100 percent, absolutely done. Unless of course a few years go by, your book is popular, and the publisher wants to do a new expanded edition.

This may be a time that you make the decision to abandon your project. That's fine. The thrill of holding your book in your hand has been realized. And it is a thrill. This is my second book in print and I'm hooked. I also have a secret for surviving the "What, I'm not really done yet?" upsets.

I celebrate. Believe me, it helps. I celebrate every time I think I'm done even though I know I'm really not. I celebrate the stages. On this book alone, one bottle at a time, I've probably had a case of champagne. It doesn't have to be expensive French. Spanish bubbly for seven dollars works just fine. I take out my flute glasses and toast myself. I worked hard. I made it to another goal. Whoo-hoo. Relax and bathe in the glow of literary success.

Then the next morning I go back to work.

Even if this book is on the bookstore shelf and there is nothing to do now, I'm a writer. I write. There is always another project to push through the stages, from thought, to manuscript, to publishing hell, to our audience. It's wonderful. It's painful. It's hard work.

y to you new kids.
many writers who
itors aren't aware of
rchies and cutthroat

TRUTH #31

MANY OF US WON'T MAKE IT

In 1776 Thomas Paine wrote, "These are the times that try men's souls." It would seem that times haven't changed all that much. Today, our writing souls are constantly being challenged. Our appetite for success and desire for recognition from our peers grow stronger with every project we complete. Few writers, if any, first put quill to paper for financial gain. A life of writing that makes an imprint on our culture we live in, is what millions of us aspire to. Long for.

You may be wondering where I am right now. I'm still networking my butt off. Still socializing with writers, managers, editors, and producers. I'm not exactly where I want to be yet, but I am working on it. And I'm still at the keys too. With every chapter or scene, I get closer to achieving my dreams. Fantasies of *New York Times* best-sellers still play between my ears, but not as often. There is simply no time to daydream. The pages are piling up on my desk and there is still so much work to do!

So to succeed in this sometimes overwhelming endeavor, we must begin by being open to success. Take these truths and let them guide you to your future. This is not an easy business. You have to write well and be smart about the choices you make.

But there are wonderful possibilities here too.

SOME OF US WILL MAKE IT. MAY ONE OF THEM BE YOU!

SPECIAL THANKS TO...

- Jerrol LeBaron of Inktip.com, for the list of genres.
  http://www.inktip.com
- Professor Gabriel Robins, for his quotations collection.
  Copyright 1994–2004.
  http://www.cs.virginia.edu/~robins/quotes.html
- Elizabeth Lyon.

r attended a writing
ok signing or literary

232   Some Writers Deserve to Starve

ript, and instead of
event inspired, you

A FEW WORDS
ON DEVELOPING CRAFT...

At conferences, I'm often asked to recommend books on writing. It's a difficult task. When it comes to some of my favorites, not every book is suited for every writer. Earlier in this book I mentioned that we as writers all evolve at our own pace.

My evolution began with the Writer's Digest Book Club. Back then, everything from travel writing to penning mysteries and Hollywood scripts appealed to me. At that time I really didn't have a focus, but I had a lot of desire. Consequently, I bought a lot of books. Some of them I read cover to cover. Others, the turkeys, got recycled. The rest sat around with bookmarks in them—I'd read the section I needed most, then promise myself I'd read the rest of the book later (ha!). Eventually these experiments yielded a direction.

I could use this page to write an exhaustive list of the books I've found helpful, but instead I'll opt to keep things simple.

1. If you're like me, and several styles of writing appeal to you, experiment until you find your direction.

2. When you find it, you really only need two books: a dictionary and *The Synonym Finder* by J.I. Rodale.

Beyond this, the best book I've ever read on writing craft is *Beyond Style: Mastering the Finer Points of Writing* (Writer's Digest Books, 1988). I keep this book by my computer and continue to use it on a regular basis. It's out of print now, but if you're lucky enough to happen upon a copy in a secondhand bookstore or through an online bookseller, snap it up. As far as developing craft goes, it is my very personal opinion that this book is one of the most worthwhile investments you will ever make.

When you are in the
of getting people to
creative endeavors is
climb Everest with a

WEB SITES AND RESOURCES

Must-Visit Web Sites

- www.publishersweekly.com
  Publishers Weekly is a trade magazine covering the book publishing industry.

- www.publisherslunch.com
  Publishers Lunch is a free weekday newsletter that's another must-read. The more extensive package—that you have to pay for—is at www. publishersmarketplace.com.

- www.aar-online.org
  Home of the Association of Authors' Representatives, a professional organization for agents.

Informational Resources

- http://shawguides.com
  ShawGuides keeps tabs on more than 1,500 writing conferences.

- www.anotherealm.com/prededitors
  Preditors & Editors posts warnings and recommendations of publishers, agents, and services related to writers.

- www.aaupnet.org
  Home of the Association of American University Presses.

- www.wga.org
  Writers Guild of America. Register your scripts here.

- www.mediabistro.com
  MediaBistro features interviews with publishing insiders, job boards, and writing classes.

- www.fundsforwriters.com
  Lists grants for writers.

- www.sfwa.org
  Home of Science Fiction & Fantasy Writers of America, known for "Writer Beware" alerts that charge agents/editors with wrongdoing.

Blogs

Blogs are great for getting a daily fix of publishing/media news and always come with a dose of attitude. Try these to start.

- MobyLives
  www.mobylives.com

- Blog of a Bookslut
  www.bookslut.com/blog

- Booksquare
  www.booksquare.com

- Maud Newton
  http://maudnewton.com/blog

When you are in the
of getting people to

creative endeavors is
climb Everest with a

- Cup of Chica
  http://www.nchicha.com

General Literary/Media News

- www.booktrade.info/index.php.
  BookTrade is a weekday e-newsletter round-up of all the book publishing news from a UK perspective.

- www.goodreports.net
  A Canadian Web site devoted to publishing news and trends.

- www.aldaily.com
  Arts & Letters Daily, a running compilation of the most interesting arts and letters articles from around the world. Academic slant.

- www.artsjournal.com
  Arts Journal is similar to Arts & Letters Daily, but with category divisions and accompanying blogs.

feel 1
are o
outsi
ing i
your
cessf
lishe
frien
acqu
es? E
ever
ed a
confe
book
or lit
gath
know
that
have
manu
and i
of lea
the e
inspi
wind
ing i
dated
seem
insur
able
peopl
are a
in th
It doe

not.
lishir

INDEX

. When you are in the
of getting people to

creative endeavors is
climb Everest with a

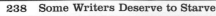

AVOID STARVATION WITH THESE OTHER FINE WRITER'S DIGEST BOOKS!

The Writer's Book of Wisdom
by Steven Goldsberry
ISBN 1-58297-292-3, hardcover, 224 pages, #10940-K

Author Steven Goldsberry teaches 101 concise—and proven— techniques on everything from tone to characterization that will get you writing immediately.

Page After Page
by Heather Sellers
ISBN 1-58297-312-1, hardcover, 240 pages, #10948-K

Ninety percent of beginning writers stop practicing their craft before they have a chance to discover their talents. This essential and encouraging guide will help you build a writing life and not give up.

Dictionary of Disagreeable English
by Robert Hartwell Fiske
ISBN 1-58297-313-X, paperback, 352 pages, #10949-K

This curmudgeon's compendium of excruciatingly correct grammar lays bare the mistakes we all make every day.

These and other fine Writer's Digest books are available at your local bookstore, online supplier, or by calling 1-800-448-0915.

. When you are in the
of getting people to

creative endeavors is
climb Everest with a